The New Creation Code

Reclaiming the Mystical Heart of Christianity

Cleveland Orville McLeish, MTS

Paperback ISBN **978-1-965635-53-7**
Hardback ISBN **978-1-965635-54-4**

Published in 2025
By
HCP Book Publishing
197 Victoria Rose Boulevard
Mount View Estate
Spanish Town
Jamaica W. I.
www.clevelandomcleish.com

Cover Design by getcovers.com

Foreword i

There are moments in the unfolding of spiritual history when a voice rises from among the sons—a sound not born of ambition, but of encounter. The New Creation Code by my beloved spiritual son, Cleveland Orville McLeish, is such a voice. It carries the resonance of one who has not merely studied truth but walked into it—one who has wrestled with mystery until the dawn broke and light clothed his words.

I have watched Cleveland grow through the quiet fires of transformation. His writing, once instructional, has now become incarnational—an expression of a man who has discovered that revelation is not information but participation. In this book, he invites us beyond doctrines into divine DNA—beyond systems of belief into the architecture of being that Yeshua Himself unveiled when He said, **"Behold, I make all things new." (Revelation 21:5).**

This work is a sacred key, turning open the hidden door between what we confess and what we embody. It summons the reader to remember that new creation is not a future hope but a present ontology—a living, breathing state of existence that flows from union with Christ. As St. Athanasius declared, *"God became man so that man might become godlike."* Here, Cleveland stands in that same river of revelation, reminding us that redemption is not simply escape from sin but re-entry into divine consciousness.

Reading this book, one does not feel instructed so much as awakened. The cadence of its insight calls forth the primordial memory of Eden—the garden within where humanity first heard the Voice walking in the cool of the day. It is not a manual but a mirror, reflecting the divine image we have too long forgotten under the rubble of religion and routine.

In the lineage of the mystics—Origen's vision of deification, Gregory of Nyssa's ascent into endless becoming, the Coptic desert fathers' cry for inner fire, the Russian saints' theology of divine light—The New Creation Code stands as a continuation of that luminous stream. It whispers to us that to be human in Christ is to be the meeting point of heaven and earth, the breathing intersection of Word and flesh.

Cleveland's writing here is not an echo; it is an emergence. It belongs to a generation of sons and daughters awakening to their inheritance, hearing again the divine rhythm that beats beneath creation: Christ in you, the hope of glory. (Colossians 1:27).

To those who read these pages, I offer this charge: do not read quickly. Let each sentence baptize you into remembrance. Let each revelation reorder your reality. For this book is not simply read—it is entered.

May the same Spirit who hovered over the waters at the beginning hover over your soul as you journey through these words. May you emerge not merely informed, but transformed—not merely awakened, but reborn into awareness.

Welcome, beloved, to The New Creation Code.

Welcome back to the Garden.

—Dr. Adonijah Ogbonnaya, PhD
Author and Teacher

For those who know there is more…

Foreword ii

This book is truly a revelation from God. *The New Creation Code* is transformational and convicting to the soul, whether saved or not. Cleveland McLeish has landed on a topic of immense importance—reclaiming our true identity. His journey through reclaiming the mystical heart of Christianity will land the reader squarely in complete union with ABBA and in direct conflict with the religious. Jesus, speaking to His disciples, said: **"Because it is given unto you to know the mysteries of the kingdom of heaven, but to them it is not given." (Matthew 13:11 - KJV).**

We must come to know that we're dealing with a complex Being—called the God of all creation. Only those who are not only born of the Spirit, but who are willing to grow in the Spirit, can understand spiritual things. Even though it has been made known, as the Apostle Paul writes: **"He has made known to us the mystery of his will, according to his purpose, which he set forth in Christ." (Ephesians 1:9 - ESV).** Understanding who we are is very important to becoming who God has created us to be. In this book, the author does an excellent job of pointing us to our true identity, whilst separating the righteous from the profane.

As I read this book, I asked myself this question: *What could motivate a man to write a book like this?* I found the answers in between the pages of this book. As I read the manuscript, I could feel a deep longing for union with God and for oneness with the Spirit. We're living in a generation that is void of the Spirit of God being manifested in His true essence, as we have wholeheartedly chosen the fake over the genuine—entertainment over empowerment, a feel-good experience over a deep encounter with God. This book, *The New Creation Code*, has been written to realign us to the Father's original plan for mankind. I wholeheartedly recommend this book to every believer. It is guaranteed to awaken the God-man locked in your DNA, which has been crying out, "There's got to be more to life than this!" It will change you, as it has done for me.

—**Apostle Dino Nicholas**
No Limits Ministries International - Canada

Therefore if any person is [ingrafted] in Christ (the Messiah)
he is a new creation (a new creature altogether); the old
[previous moral and spiritual condition] has passed away.
Behold, the fresh and new has come!
—(2 Corinthians 5:17 - AMPC).

"The Christian of the future will be a mystic or he will not exist at all."

—Karl Rahner

Preface

There are books that explain faith, and then there are books that unveil it. The *New Creation Code* is the latter. This work is not merely about Christianity, it is an inward journey, a return to something primal, radiant, and alive within the soul of the believer. It is a daring excavation of the Christian soul, buried under centuries of dogma, denominational enclosures, empty rituals and theological scaffolding.

This book is not for the comfortably religious, nor for those content to worship at the altars of certainty. It is for the spiritually hungry, for those who feel the subterranean tremors of divine longing deep beneath the surface of their Sunday rituals. It is for those who have sat in pews yet felt exiled from Eden, who have read the scriptures yet ached for the Word behind the words.

Here you will not be handed a system of belief but invited into an eternal mystery as it slowly unfolds. You will not find neatly wrapped answers, but doorways—thin places where heaven brushes against earth and eternity whispers through time. Like the mystics before us, Julian of Norwich, whose soul saw all things held in the palm of God *"like a little thing,"* or Meister Eckhart, who spoke of the birth of the Word in the soul, we are not here to understand God as much as to encounter God.

The New Creation Code does not treat Christianity as a moral code, a tribal identity, or an ideology to be weaponized. Rather, it is a call to remember—to return. It points us back to the Garden, before the first altar, before the first sacrifice, before the law and the prophets, before our divisions and denominations; it points us back to that moment when man walked with God, not as a grovelling sinner but as an image-bearer, not as one earning love, but as one already loved.

St. Gregory of Nyssa once said, *"The soul's desire is to see God, but the more it sees, the more it desires, for it stretches forever into God's infinite mystery."* This book stretches likewise, not as a treatise but as a trajectory, not as a conclusion, but as an awakening.

If you have ever suspected that the Christianity we inherited is not the fullness Christ intended—if you've ever dared to believe there is more—you are not alone. You were made to sense more, to carry more, to become more. What you long for is not new, but ancient. What calls to you is not foreign, but familiar.

This is your invitation to follow the tremors back to the Source, to listen again to the sound of the Spirit who hovered over the waters, to awaken the divine code written into your very being.

Come let us rediscover the mystical heart of Christianity, not as theologians dissecting a doctrine, but as lovers returning home.

Table of Contents

The New Creation Code

I am about to do something I have never seen in my many years as an author and book publisher. I want to start with the end in mind—though it's a bit jumbled and fragmented—because this summative narrative needs to be heard before any introduction or chapters. These are my own musings, shaped by what I have accepted as truth.

I have appeared on several platforms with clergy, and I noticed a pervasive theme (consciousness): *spirituality has been defaulted to the demonic, occultic movements are credited with power, and believers have been reduced to powerless rescuers whose sole purpose is to drag people from hell without bringing them into deep spiritual maturity.* We focus on evangelism yet often fail at discipleship. This is not biblical.

The church's mandate is clear. But God's original purpose for mankind—to rule and reign—is overlooked. In our narrative, God is the hero; man is the recipient. Salvation has become the end. But in truth, salvation restores man to his created purpose as image-bearers (Image Dei) with divine authority.

I want to address the fallen consciousness and the bad theology that have replaced true Christ-consciousness. We profess a form of godliness yet deny its power (see 2 Timothy 3:5). We fallback to religion—rulebooks, rituals, reputations—while ignoring relationship.

Who fell? Not God. He never forgets His identity or abdicates His glory. Man did. We ask, *"Who is God?"* But the more essential question is: *"Who is man?"* David asked it centuries ago: *"What is man?" (Psalm 8:4 - NKJV).* This is the question that has ravaged a perfect reality and harmony that once existed as even angels are stupefied by this created being who was made to host the God of the universe.

I will summarize God's redemptive narrative—without quoting every scripture—because these reflections require deep study. Yet underlying everything are two forces we must avoid:

1. **Babylonian systems:** Humanity's attempt to reach or manipulate heaven apart from God.

2. **Doctrines of demons:** Deceptive frameworks that blend truth with error (see 1 Timothy 4:1).

Our theology and interpretation of scripture are influenced by our consciousness—our spiritual lens. When Jesus came, people stared at the truth and didn't recognize Him. We do the same today. Before we can receive truth, we need a renewed mind or what is called "spiritual enlightenment" (see Romans 12:2).

GOD AND MAN: POSITION RESTORED

God is everything—the "All in All" (see Colossians 3:11). Even non-believers sense His existence; denial proves recognition.

We see man as nothing. A blob in reality. A vapor that appears and disappears momentarily. We refer to ourselves as worthless, bastards, worms… less than. The repercussions of this thought process then elevate spiritual beings, including demons, above a man's true value. The value of man has been significantly diminished, even though God proves our value by becoming human. This mindset gets even more extremely dangerous when we demonize the spiritual realm, which is the consciousness the church has functioned under for centuries. We frame our reality based on what we can interact with in the physical world, and anything coming out of the spiritual world is, by default, demonic, even though most of it is God.

Our positioning of man is skewed. We need a new vocabulary and new spiritual grammar to recalibrate our consciousness before time ends.

A COSMIC BLUEPRINT

"In the beginning, God created the heavens and the earth." (Genesis 1:1 – NKJV).

'Heavens' is plural. The Bible reveals a first and third heaven (see 2 Corinthians 12:2), and tradition speaks of up to seven—layered realities, some physical, some spiritual, woven through time.

Creation is God fashioning a space within Himself—a divine theater for being.

God is Spirit, not "a spirit." He created a physical world needing a physical steward—a human made in His image, to rule and subdue (see Genesis 1:26–28). Man was originally clothed in light, not shame.

Some describe pre-fall man as a "light being"—radiant until sin eclipsed that glory. As Augustine and modern mystics

24

like A.W. Tozer suggest, sin didn't just corrupt us, it diminished our identity.

FREEDOM AND FREE WILL

Man was created in time; angels exist outside time.

There have been several foundational falls:

- ❧ The "son of the morning" (Lucifer), the cherub who fell (see Ezekiel 28:14–15).

- ❧ A third of angels siding with him (see Revelation 12:4).

- ❧ Man's fall, which fractured creation and plunged us under it.

- ❧ The Watchers' fall—angelic beings mating with human women, birthing Nephilim. Their rebellion triggered the flood judgment in Genesis.

These fallen beings—human, angelic, demonic—reflect the misuse of free will. It reminds us that everything wrong in creation relates to "not-God" choices.

REDEMPTION AND RE-CREATION

Despite the disorder, God loved man too much to leave him broken. Redeeming us was a cosmic move, not just personal salvation. It's spiritual duality: death to sin, resurrection to divine nature (see 1 Corinthians 15:22 and Romans 6:4–5).

Fallen angels are not demons. As a matter of fact, the Bible says there are fallen angels who are in chains somewhere awaiting judgment. Fallen angels are still angels in nature and function, just fallen. That's why they can appear to you as an angel of light.

Demons are disembodied fragments seeking new hosts. Genesis 6's hybridity sparked chaos—flooded remnant but left spiritual debris.

The first demonic undertaking was the Tower of Babel (see Genesis 11): man attempting to breach heaven independent of God. This rejection of relationship for rule birthed Babylon, a spiritual system of man-made identity.

God called man to union and reign, not to remain victims of fallen realities. But because of the falls, we have layers of travail to contend with.

Man was created above angels, below God. Angels marvel at his potential (see Psalm 8). The fall submerged him. Redemption restores him, but only by faith during time.

Remember: those out of time—angels removed themselves and have no hope of redemption. Only humans born in time can repent and be remade. It means that when time cease to exist in the future, any human being that falls after we have been glorified will stay fallen. There is always the possibility of falling unless God removes our free will.

So man matters. He is the only image-bearer. Angels are curious; demons seek to enslave. Everything begins and ends with man. If corruption erupted in humanity, restoration must emanate from humanity. So God became human (see Hebrews 2:14–18).

NOW IS OUR TIME

Yet, many churches await Jesus' return to fix things. That's bad theology. Jesus already came. We already have the Holy Spirit, the gifts of the Spirit, the written Word.

We have all we need to set creation right—in union with Him—not in the future but now. To wait idly is a spiritual misalignment.

A human can go in three directions:

⌐ Be used by God.

⌐ Be used by fallen beings.

⌐ Do their own thing.

This third option sounds plausible, until we realize everything happens through—and because of—man. He murders, sexualizes, corrupts. But only man can bring light into darkness. So God took human form.

David asked: **"What is man that You are mindful of him?" (Psalm 8:4 - NKJV).** He recognized divine significance, even amid dust. He saw something beyond fallen constraints, something restored and exalted in God Himself.

THE NEW CREATION — OUR DESTINY

God in Jesus became the second Adam, the fully divine-human prototype—the path to our restoration. He healed bodies, calmed storms, multiplied scarcity, and walked on water, all in His humanity.

He said we would do greater things (see John 14:12) because we are not "partial" but destined for full metamorphosis—

fueled not by self-effort, but by a renewed mind engaging the mystery of God.

God reveals Himself to seekers with pure hearts (see Psalm 25:14). The Apostle John affirmed it: **"Beloved, now we are children of God; and it has not yet been revealed what we shall be, but we know that when He is revealed, we shall be like Him, for we shall see Him as He is." (1 John 3:2 - NKJV).**

The reality of the Image Dei is an already-but-not-yet. What Jesus reveals is already-but-is-yet-to-be even though it already-is. Such is the language of eternity in the context of time. We peel away the mystery of the "man in God" layer by layer until all lays bare.

A man is not defined by the fall but by his capacity to rise again. The righteous falls seven times but he rises again.

Man is the crowning glory of God's marvellous creation. One soul equates to the value of the whole world. For one, God would have still become a man and endured the shame, suffering and death at the hands of His own creation. By one man, the world fell into sin and by one Man, the world now has access to restoration.

When Moses asked to see the glory of God, he was shown the creation of man. Man fell short of the glory of God when he disobeyed God. That glory is restored whenever a new soul is born into the kingdom. The light and glory of God expands when a child of God is born from above. This is the mystery of salvation and the power of the gospel. If every human being on earth is born again, there would be no darkness. The world would be reset to the beginning when God said, **"Let there be light."**

But this depends on our self-view. If we believe we are separate, disconnected, small, powerless—darkness wins. Zion must awaken. The church must embrace mystical enlightenment and move beyond religion into revolution.

Christianity is not a creed; it is a movement. It is not a structure; it is a people. Christianity is not a code of conduct; it is a way of life. When practiced authentically, it topples systems and ushers in the manifest presence of God.

That is the New Creation Code: a call to restore what was lost, so that **God and man** resume unity, not as priest and altar, but as co-heirs and co-creators in Christ (see Romans 8:17).

I believe even when time dissolves, the greatest revelation will be that there was never anything but God, for He is the All in All, the Everything in Everything (see Ephesians 1:23).

So let us now begin to peel back the layers of the New Creation Code.

Introduction

There is a question that has long haunted the quiet moments of my meditation, a question that does not leave me alone. It presses against the edges of inherited belief and pierces through well-worn theology. The question is this: *"What if Christianity is not what we have made it?"*

I did not foresee that this question seldom asked could translate into a lifelong purpose. I have found myself pursuing an answer to this question for more than a decade, and the answers I have encountered are quite staggering. Profound actually, and without even realizing it, my language started to change, and I noticed the weird looks when I finish talking and took note of the silence that ensued because one could not figure out how to respond to my musings before I realized that I was speaking in a different context—a different language.

The idea of religion was illusive. I saw beyond the everyday rituals of a Christian to something deeper, something more spiritual…a calling that not many seem to answer. It was a gentle whisper, yet an invitation to all, *"Come up higher. Enter the unknown. Dive into the mystery that awaits the seekers of God."* Then the religious layers of Christianity began to be peeled back, bit by bit, revealing something even more authentic than our feeble attempts to reach God by works; I saw a call to relationship. More questions emerged.

What if the church was never meant to be an institution managed by human hierarchy, but a living, breathing organism—Christ's own body animated by divine breath? What if the gospel is not a formula for escaping earth, but the unveiling of heaven on earth, within us and around us? What if being "born again" is not the finish line of spiritual arrival, but the genesis of a cosmic reinstatement—our re-entry into a divine narrative far more ancient and glorious than we've dared to imagine?

Are we bold enough to chase these questions into the heart of God?

Are you?

God has gifted us with intellect, not as an idol to worship, but as a compass to navigate the mystery. The Holy Spirit is not afraid of our questions. He invites them. As Saint

Augustine once prayed, *"Lord, you have made us for yourself, and our heart is restless until it rests in you."* Restlessness, when rightly channelled, is a sign that the soul is waking up.

We must not fear our yearning to probe the depth of spiritual reality. After all, deception always masquerades as truth. From the beginning, the serpent asked, **"Has God indeed said...?" (Genesis 3:1 - NKJV).** That seed of doubt has echoed through history, causing humanity to distort truth and manufacture reality on its own terms. Even Babel was built by those who sought the heights of heaven without the intimacy of God (see Genesis 11). Could it be that much of what we call "Christianity" today is our own modern Babel—an edifice of religion built apart from relational presence?

The New Creation Code was not written as a theological treatise, nor as a critique of tradition. I wrote it as a scholar, and as a son. A son who, like the mystics of old, is trying to remember, not merely what I believe, but who I am.

I am not searching for "my truth" or defending doctrines handed down to me without examination. I am searching for The Truth—the Logos who became flesh and dwelt among us (see John 1:14). I am willing to lose everything I

35

thought I knew if it means gaining Christ. Like Paul, I count all things as loss *"that I may know Him and the power of His resurrection." (Philippians 3:10 - NKJV).*

I have wrestled with scripture. I was not attempting to master it, but to be mastered by it. I have walked with modern day Christian mystics, and have dreamed to walk with the likes of Teresa of Ávila, who wrote of the "interior castle" of the soul where God abides; with Thomas Merton, who warned us that we can spend our whole life climbing a ladder of success only to find it leaning against the wrong wall. I have prayed in silence, not to escape sound, but to listen beneath it. I have listened to the ache of generations disillusioned by religion yet still drawn to the presence of God.

Here, you will not find an attempt to appease orthodoxy, nor to wage war against it. My aim is not to offend, but to awaken. If this book unsettles your comfort but stirs your spirit, it has served its purpose.

This is not about rebellion. This is about return—Return to purpose. Return to presence. Return to union. Return to relationship. It is a call to remember, because we have forgotten. We have ignored the One knocking at the door to

THE NEW CREATION CODE

our hearts so we can chase our own fantasies and live the Christian life on our own terms.

"Come back, wanderer, come back home."—This is the quiet refrain of the Holy Spirit, echoing through every secret longing. There is a part of us that knows the truth and gently prods us to sit up and pay attention, but this part of us can be held captive by our will. It can be silenced by the noise of our own selfish desires.

The journey begins where it always should have—not in a pew, but in the heart of God. For before religion, before law, before even sin, we were created for union. Created to walk with God in the cool of the day (see Genesis 3:8).

"The secret [of the wise counsel] of the Lord is for those who fear Him, and He will let them know His covenant and reveal to them [through His word] its [deep, inner] meaning." (Psalm 25:14 - AMP).

If you will dare to enter the secret, you will find that God has not hidden truth *from* you but *for* you.

We journey now into the deep and the high, into the mystery and the wonder. We ask hard questions, and we must be prepared for unsettling answers.

If it is true—as scripture says—*"Eye has not seen, nor ear heard, nor have entered into the heart of man the things which God has prepared for those who love Him." (1 Corinthians 2:9 - NKJV),* then not even this book—nor any brilliant volume ever written—can fully articulate the divine dream God has for His people.

But still—we pursue.

We pursue because there is something in us that knows we were made for more. We pursue, as St. John of the Cross did, in the dark night of the soul, trusting that even in unknowing, we are being led by Love. We pursue, not perfection, but Presence.

And perhaps, if grace allows, the veil will part just enough for us to shed the illusions we have carried, and walk again with God in Spirit and Truth.

Let the journey begin.

Chapter 1

The Church Today

I am a member of the body of Christ, the church, and I am unashamedly critical of her. It's not because I am against her, but because I am for her. I critique not from the outside but from within, as a committed participant, lover of scripture, and scholar of the sacred text. And I confess: I struggle to reconcile what I read in the Word with what I witness in the modern church.

The Bible is no ordinary book. It is alive. It is prophetic. It is, as the mystics say, a "thin place" between heaven and earth. Within its pages are not merely moral principles, but portals—windows into other dimensions of divine-human interaction. From creation to the fall, from Eden to Revelation, the Bible brims with awe, wonder, and mystery. It is unapologetically mystical and wildly supernatural.

One professor once reflected on the strange encounter between King Saul, the dead prophet Samuel, and the witch of Endor. His remark? *"That was wild. What was happening there?"* Then he moved on. That moment—where the boundary between life and death is pierced—is debated endlessly. Was it truly Samuel? A demonic impersonation? Scripture doesn't spoon-feed. It invites us into mystery, and mystery is something the modern church has forgotten how to handle.

What we often do, mistakenly, is reduce scripture to our level of human understanding. We domesticate it. We strip it of its divine tension. We do the same to the church. In our quest for order, we have created a form of faith that looks more like the synagogues of Jesus' day than the upper room of Acts.

The early followers of Jesus didn't merely "go to church"— they became the church. They were part of a movement called The Way. They were not institutional—they were incarnational. But what we call "church" today has devolved into routine, rhetoric, and religion.

Prayer has become a monologue—a performance of words rather than communion with God.

Worship is often entertainment, stripped of awe. Lights, fog machines, emotional crescendos—yet hearts remain untouched.

The Fivefold Ministry—apostles, prophets, evangelists, pastors, and teachers—has been largely abandoned or misunderstood. Many churches are run like corporations, not communities of grace.

We no longer fast. We rarely read the Bible outside of Sunday mornings. We forsake corporate fellowship for livestreams and convenience. We do not love one another as Christ commanded; instead, we judge harshly, gossip quickly, manipulate subtly, and prioritize self-gain.

Sexual immorality—whether fornication, adultery, or homosexuality—is now normalized, even affirmed, without any true conviction or call to holiness. We have traded repentance for relevance.

We disregard the Seven Spirits of God—wisdom, understanding, counsel, might, knowledge, fear of the Lord, and the Spirit of the Lord (see Isaiah 11:2). We don't teach about angels. In fact, most spiritual phenomena are instantly labelled as "demonic," as if the diabolic entities have more authority over the spiritual realm than God does.

We don't believe in the supernatural—miracles, signs, and wonders have become passé. And in a world drowning in unbelief, we have abandoned the very evidences that God gave us to demonstrate His reality. *How will people believe without miracles?* The early church didn't debate that—they simply healed the sick, cast out demons, and raised the dead.

We don't take daily communion, although Jesus said, **"Do this in remembrance of Me" (Luke 22:19 - NKJV).** Not weekly. Not quarterly. Daily. As mystic Evelyn Underhill once wrote, *"Worship is not an escape from the world but a penetration into the heart of it."*

This, sadly, is not the radiant church Christ is returning for. What we are left with is a religion—a form of godliness that denies the power (see 2 Timothy 3:5). And then we wonder, in our conferences and committees, *"Why don't we see what they saw in the Book of Acts?"*

The answer is clear: we do not believe what they believed. We do not live how they lived.

Jesus rebuked the synagogue leaders of His day because they were guilty of the same things we are. Their prayers were performances. Their reading of Torah lacked heart. They tithed but ignored mercy. They fasted but exploited the poor.

They worshipped a God they didn't truly know (see John 4:22). And when the very One the scriptures pointed to appeared in flesh—Jesus—they didn't recognize Him.

If we are not careful, history will repeat itself. Jesus warned in Matthew 7:22–23, **"I can see it now—at the Final Judgment thousands strutting up to me and saying, 'Master, we preached the Message, we bashed the demons, our God-sponsored projects had everyone talking.' And do you know what I am going to say? 'You missed the boat. All you did was use me to make yourselves important. You don't impress me one bit.'"** (MSG).

St. John of the Cross once warned that the greatest danger to the church was not persecution from outside but pride and blindness from within.

This is the hour for the church to awaken—to return to her mystical origins, her supernatural DNA. She must reclaim what was always hers: intimacy with God, purity of devotion, power through the Spirit, and authority as the body of Christ.

We are not called to mimic culture; we are called to transform it. We are not called to entertain; we are called to embody Christ. If the church does not awaken to her identity, calling, and spiritual inheritance, she may not recognize her Lord, Master and King when He comes again.

Chapter 2

What It Means to Be a Christian

To be a Christian is not merely to subscribe to a belief system, but to participate in divine life— God's life, pulsing in us and through us. It is not allegiance to an institution or assent to doctrine, but a surrender to a living relationship. Christianity, in its truest and most mystical form, is not the worship of Christ from a distance, but the indwelling of Christ within us— *"Christ in you, the hope of glory" (Colossians 1:27 - NKJV).* It is not Christ merely for us, but Christ as us, working through every fiber of our being.

Modern Christianity has often been flattened into a system of creeds, codes, and customs—well-meaning but insufficient constructs that can all too easily veil the wild, living presence of God. The early followers of Jesus knew something radically different. They walked in what Paul called a "new creation" (see 2 Corinthians 5:17)—a complete reorientation of reality through participation in the life, death, and resurrection of Christ. This reality is now embedded in the DNA of the born-again believer.

"This means that anyone who belongs to Christ has become a new person. The old life is gone; a new life has begun!" (2 Corinthians 5:17 - NLT).

This is not a play on words or some sort of metaphor. This is the truth: We are *new*. Christianity is about union with God. It is the mystery that the early church called theosis— the idea that we are not only reconciled to God but invited into participation with His very nature. As 2 Peter 1:4 declares: *"For by these He has bestowed on us His precious and magnificent promises [of inexpressible value], so that by them you may escape from the immoral freedom that is in the world because of disreputable desire, and become sharers of the divine nature." (AMP).*

This is no metaphor. It is mystical reality. In other words, union is not theoretical; it is experiential. Christianity is not about striving to reach God but awakening to the God who already dwells within.

The real question, then, is not *"Do you go to church?"* or *"Do you believe in the right doctrine?"* The real question is: *"Has Christ been formed in you?"* As Paul wrote, **"My little children, for whom I labor in birth again until Christ is formed in you." (Galatians 4:19 - NKJV).** This is the ultimate goal.

We have confused attending church with being the church. A "Christian" may go to a building weekly, but a child of God understands they are the temple.

"You realize, don't you, that you are the temple of God, and God himself is present in you?" (1 Corinthians 3:16 - MSG).

The distinction is critical. We are not spectators of a divine performance. We are participants in the divine life. We are not mere believers—we are partakers.

Paul says this beautifully in Ephesians 2:19-22: **"You're no longer wandering exiles. This kingdom of faith is now your home country... God is building a home. He's using us all—irrespective of how we got here—in what he is building... a holy temple built by God, all of us built into it, a temple in which God is quite at home." (MSG).**

To be a Christian is to become aware that we are already entangled with the Divine. It is not a status we achieve, but a truth we awaken to. As Thomas Merton wrote, *"We are already one. But we imagine that we are not. And what we have to recover is our original unity."*

The title "Christian" was first given in Antioch (see Acts 11:26) and was likely used as a form of mockery. It meant *"little Christs."* But ironically, the name contains a profound truth: we are not merely followers of Christ—we are those in whom Christ continues to walk the earth.

Yet, we live in a culture of separation consciousness—a false belief that God is *"out there"* and we are *"down here."* But Paul said plainly: ***"In Him we live and move and have our being." (Acts 17:28 - NKJV).*** It is not enough to know who we are and whose we are; we must also know where we are. We are located *"in Christ, in God."*

God is not distant. He is the very ground of our being. Too often, "Christianity" has attached purpose to appointments—titles, roles, and positions within the church. But divine purpose does not originate in human recognition. You were not born to fill a church roster; you were born to fulfil a divine design.

Your purpose is encoded in your spiritual DNA. It predates your pastor's approval and your denomination's hierarchy. Jeremiah 1:5 reminds us: *"Before I formed you in the womb I knew you [and approved of you as My chosen instrument], and before you were born I consecrated you [to Myself as My own]." (AMP).*

This means your calling is eternal. Whether or not you're "appointed" by men, you are already anointed and appointed by God. You were born into this world with a purpose coded into your very being. This is what is lost when a human being denies Christ. While God can still use them to fulfil particular tasks, they never attain to the fullness of their call.

The child of God doesn't need a title to function in their purpose. A title may clarify your role, but it does not define your identity. You are the church. You are a temple of the Holy Spirit. You are a carrier of the kingdom.

Jesus never said, *"Build a religion in my name."* He said, *"Follow Me."* Not to a church building, but to a cross, to death, and into resurrection life.

"The church you see is not peripheral to the world; the world is peripheral to the church. The church is Christ's

body, in which he speaks and acts, by which he fills everything with his presence." (Ephesians 1:22–23 - MSG).

Let us be clear: a church record with your name on it does not guarantee your name is recorded in the Lamb's Book of Life. As Jesus warned in Matthew 7:21: *"Not everyone who says to Me, 'Lord, Lord,' shall enter the kingdom of heaven, but he who does the will of My Father in heaven."* *(NKJV).*

To be a Christian is more than belief. It is transformation. More than attending. It is abiding. More than knowing about God. It is knowing God and being known by Him.

Christianity is not about becoming more religious, it's about becoming more real—more human, more alive, more unified with the divine image you were always meant to bear. It is not about doing. It is about being and becoming.

Because God is, we are. Because Christ lives, we too live. And in that mystery is the essence of the new creation.

Let us not settle for a version of Christianity that merely informs our intellect or checks our moral boxes. Let us walk into the mystery that transforms the soul, renews the mind, and reveals Christ in us, not merely to us.

This is what it means to be a Christian.

Chapter 3

The Beginning: Humanity Before Religion

I n the beginning, God did not create Christians. He created humans—image-bearers. Adam and Eve were glorious beings not merely designed to worship, but to reflect, to co-create, to govern and host God's presence. This is the forgotten genesis of our identity.

Genesis 1:26–28 says: **"Then God said, 'Let Us make man in Our image, according to Our likeness; let them have dominion...' So God created man in His own image; in the image of God He created him; male and female He created them. Then God blessed them..."** (NKJV).

This speaks to both form and function. It is not just resemblance, but relationship. The human being was formed in the Imago Dei—the image of God—not to observe God from a distance, but to be a visible expression of the Invisible within the created order.

As mystic and scholar Howard Thurman wrote, *"The hunger of the human heart for God is too deep to be satisfied with dogma. It is only satisfied when the soul touches the Eternal directly."*

From the beginning, God's intention was union—a shared dominion, a sacred partnership. Humanity was to walk with God, not as a grovelling subject but as a co-ruler, a beloved child endowed with the breath of the Divine.

"The Lord God formed man of the dust of the ground, and breathed into his nostrils the breath of life; and man became a living being." (Genesis 2:7 - NKJV).

This divine breath—the *Ruach* in Hebrew—is more than oxygen. It is divine essence—it is God as Spirit. In that moment, humanity was not given a religion. Humanity was given divine life.

Religion, as we know it, did not come about by divine design, but from human disconnection. When intimacy was fractured—when the walk in the Garden was interrupted by shame and hiding—humanity, in its fear and fragmentation, attempted to build a substitute for lost union. Religion became the architecture of distance.

It was in this rupture that religion was born, not as a revelation from God, but as a compensation for His felt absence. Altars replaced intimacy. Rituals replaced relationship. Law replaced love. We see this impulse on full display in Matthew 17:4, when Peter, upon witnessing the transfiguration of Jesus, Moses, and Elijah, blurts out:

"Lord, it is good and delightful and auspicious that we are here; if You wish, I will put up three sacred tents here—one for You, one for Moses, and one for Elijah." (AMP).

Peter instinctively tries to memorialize the moment—to contain the mystery within something manageable. But the voice from the cloud interrupts him: **"This is My beloved Son, with whom I am well-pleased and delighted! Listen to Him!"** (Matthew 17:5 - AMP).

What Peter didn't understand is what we still struggle to grasp: revelation is meant to transform us, not be enshrined by us. As modern contemplative Richard Rohr often reminds us, *"The human ego prefers something it can control, which is why religion has always been more popular than the mystical path."*

Why do we default to dogma and systems? Because mystery unsettles us. The unknown threatens our illusion of control. We define God because a defined deity is easier to manage. But in doing so, we trade the wild wonder of encounter for the safety of institutional familiarity. Over time, revelation ossifies into ritual. Encounters become doctrines. Movements become monuments. Every substitute lacks the potent power of the authentic.

In her book, the *Interior Castle*, Teresa of Ávila warns that when we refuse to move inward—into the sacred depths where God dwells within—we build false rooms for the soul to dwell in. These rooms are religious endeavours often filled with noise and presence. That's what happened in much of our spiritual tradition. We built doctrines around experience, instead of letting experiences draw us deeper into God. As T.S. Eliot once wrote, *"We had the experience but missed the meaning."*

I once had a conversation with a group of people, and we were speaking about the prophetic. I remember saying that if God opens one's eyes to see in the spirit, and they see a door, don't come from the experience and start a prophetic

THE NEW CREATION CODE

ministry, and even name it "Open Door Ministry." Instead, go through the door. Be guided by the Spirit. Allow God to lead you through that encounter so you see and hear what God is trying to show you. Too often we build ministries to encompass our brief spiritual experiences, thereby restricting, limiting or even cancelling the possibility of being changed by the encounter.

I remember sitting in seminary, where my professor—a respected New Testament scholar—made a statement that disrupted my entire theological framework. In discussing Paul's letters (which compose a large portion of the New Testament), he said: *"We must remember: Paul was not writing doctrine. He was writing letters—specific instructions to specific communities in specific situations. If Paul were writing to us today, his content would likely be very different." (paraphrased).*

That statement shook me. We often read Paul's letters as if they were carved in eternal stone, but they are deeply pastoral, contextual, and fluid. Paul was not systematizing a religion; he was responding to life. He was trying to articulate, with limited language, an unlimited reality: Christ in you. Union. Mystery.

"The mystery which has been hidden from ages and from generations, but now has been revealed to His saints." (Colossians 1:26 - NKJV).

To this day, we have not been successful in articulating the mystery of the finished work of Jesus Christ and what it means for the born-again believer. In all honesty, the reality of it must be experienced and lived not articulated. Mystics throughout history have warned us of the danger of substituting knowledge about God for knowing God. As Evelyn Underhill wrote, *"The spiritual life is not a special career involving abstraction from the world. It is the realization of the presence of God in all life."*

So what do we make of our religious structures?

They are not evil in themselves. They can be containers for presence, but they must never be confused with presence. A wineskin is only useful if it holds new wine. When the wine ferments, the skin must stretch or be replaced. Otherwise, it bursts (see Matthew 9:17).

God is always inviting us forward. Always drawing us beyond what we've known into what we have yet to experience.

To return to the Garden is not to become anti-religious. It is to become pre-religious—to rediscover the essence of who we were before we lost Him in the trees. Before shame. Before exile. Before altar or law. Our journey is a return to walking with God naked and unashamed (see Genesis 2:25). To live not by rites, but by presence. To breathe again the Ruach.

"God's readiness to give and forgive is now public. Salvation's available for everyone!" (Titus 2:11 - MSG).

This is not rebellion. This is not heresy. This is us returning home.

Chapter 4

A Gospel of Glory, Not of Escape

The modern gospel, in many circles, has been reduced to a transaction—God in exchange for comfort and faith in exchange for material blessings. It has been repackaged as a spiritual insurance policy, a guarantee of health, wealth, worldly ease and comfort. The era of the "prosperity gospel" taught that God's favor is proven by financial abundance, bodily wellness, and a life free from adversity. The consciousness of the church adapted this mindset to the point that it became the standard for Christianity. We began to see wealth as a pathway to comfort and an opportunity to indulge in our wildest fantasies.

The effect of this skewed consciousness today is our church's practice to spend millions or billions on a church edifice, and far less in developing the people of God. People are eternal investments. Buildings are not. From the days of law to our day of grace, people have been the priority in how we steward our resources in the kingdom of God. But that's not what we are talking about now.

Christianity is not an escape from problems, difficulties, trials and suffering. If suffering disqualifies divine favor, then what are we to make of Jesus—the Man of Sorrows, acquainted with grief? (see Isaiah 53:3). If comfort equals anointing, then the cross is a contradiction. But the cross is not the contradiction—it is the clarification.

"He was despised and rejected by men, a Man of sorrows and pain and acquainted with grief...Yet it was the will of the Lord to crush Him, causing Him to suffer." (Isaiah 53:3, 10 - AMP).

The true gospel is not about escape from suffering, but about glory revealed through it. It is not a parachute out of pain, but a portal through which the divine enters and transforms the human condition. Jesus did not avoid suffering—He entered it, and in so doing, transfigured it.

"So we are convinced that every detail of our lives is continually woven together to fit into God's perfect plan of bringing good into our lives..." (Romans 8:28 - MSG).

PEACE IS A PERSON, NOT A CONDITION

Peace is not the absence of storms but the presence of Christ in the midst of them. Jesus slept through a life-threatening storm (see Mark 4:38) not because He was reckless or unaware, but because He embodied peace. The storm had no authority over the One who had already stilled the storm within.

"But He was in the stern, asleep on a pillow. And they awoke Him and said, 'Teacher, do You not care that we are perishing?'" (Mark 4:38 - NKJV).

Peter, too, slept soundly in a prison cell the night before his scheduled execution (see Acts 12:6). Imagine the calmness of spirit required to sleep knowing your death was imminent. That is not natural peace—it is supernatural union. Peter had tapped into the rest of God, the same rest spoken of in Hebrews 4—a rest not found in circumstance but in trust and surrender.

"There remains therefore a rest for the people of God… Let us therefore be diligent to enter that rest…" (Hebrews 4:9, 11 - NKJV).

Rest, in the kingdom of God, is not inactivity—it is a posture of the heart. It is not circumstantial, but relational. The mystic St. John of the Cross said it like this: *"God leads every soul by a different path, but He brings them all to Himself. The path is narrow, but full of peace."*

SUCCESS IS ALIGNMENT, NOT APPLAUSE

In the kingdom, success is not measured by accumulation, achievement, or applause. It is measured by alignment—the degree to which one abides in the will of the Father. Jesus Himself declared, **"I do nothing of Myself... but what I see the Father do" (John 5:19 - NKJV).** His ministry was not defined by metrics, but by obedience and presence.

"I carry out the will of the One who sent me, not my own will." (John 5:30 – MSG).

Jesus was rejected, misunderstood, betrayed, and crucified, yet He was perfectly aligned with the heart of the Father. The notion that favor equals comfort would disqualify every apostle, every martyr, every prophet, and even Christ Himself.

Mystic Evelyn Underhill said: *"If God were small enough to be understood, He would not be big enough to be* worshipped." The life of Christ defies formula. So should the gospel.

THE GOSPEL IS INCARNATION, NOT ESCAPISM

The gospel does not lift us out of the human condition; it transfigures it from within. It is incarnation, not escapism. God did not send Christ to deliver us from the world, but to empower us to live in it as light, as salt, as new creations (see Matthew 5:13–16; 2 Corinthians 5:17).

This gospel of glory teaches us that divine life is poured into cracked vessels, and yet, somehow, the cracks become the very places where light leaks through.

"We now have this light shining in our hearts, but we ourselves are like fragile clay jars containing this great treasure..." (2 Corinthians 4:7 - NLT).

To believe that Christianity promises a life free from struggle is to miss the point of the cross. Suffering is not a sign of God's absence, but often the stage for His greatest glory. Theologian Jürgen Moltmann writes: *"God weeps with us so that we may one day laugh with Him."*

The question *"Why does a good God allow suffering?"* finds its answer not in philosophical speculation but in incarnation. God did not distance Himself from human suffering. God entered our suffering. He did not observe it from a distance; He embraced it in full.

TRANSFORMATION WITHOUT ESCAPE

Christianity is not about avoiding pain, but about being transformed within it. A woman who gives her life to Christ while in an abusive marriage may still go home to the same broken environment. Her external situation might remain unchanged, but the love she now embodies begins to reshape her inner world. This love, the very essence of Christ in her, may become a redemptive force in her home, but even if her husband never changes, she has changed, and that transformation is real and eternal.

As Thomas à Kempis wrote in The Imitation of Christ: *"Carry the cross patiently, and in the end, it will carry you."* This gospel is not a pain-free path, it is a radiant resurrection arising from ashes. It does not promise escape from the world but offers a return to the Image Dei within us, even as the world continues to burn.

"The whole creation is on tiptoe to see the wonderful sight of the sons of God coming into their own." (Romans 8:19 - PHILLIPS).

THE PURPOSE OF OUR TRANSFORMATION

Why, then, are we transformed, if not for applause or personal gain? We are transformed for the glory that is to be revealed through us.

"Yet what we suffer now is nothing compared to the glory he will reveal to us later." (Romans 8:18 - NLT).

"For our light affliction, which is but for a moment, is working for us a far more exceeding and eternal weight of glory…" (2 Corinthians 4:17 - NKJV).

This is the mystery of the gospel: God does not eliminate suffering, He redeems it. And in redeeming it, He reveals a glory that cannot be seen in ease or opulence. Glory often hides itself in broken places. That is why Christ came wrapped in swaddling cloth and crucified between thieves. And that is why the gospel still calls to us, not with the voice of escape, but with the invitation to be transfigured, to walk through fire and come out glowing with the very glory of God.

I hear it too often. When the world gets too overwhelming for believers, we begin to make prophetic declarations that Jesus is coming soon. *"Any minute now! Come, Lord Jesus!"*

echoes from the lips of those who bear the restored image of God but do not want to face a world that is lost and broken. *"Jesus is coming soon"* is good news for believers, and not so good news for the many who have not yet accepted Jesus as Lord and Savior. We carry good news, not for ourselves, but for the lost. Jesus has come. The Holy Spirit was given. We bear the good news of the kingdom of God to a world steeped in chaos. This is not a gospel of escape; this is the gospel of glory.

Chapter 5

God's Original Mandate For Humanity

When God declared, "**Let Us make man in Our image, according to Our likeness...**" (**Genesis 1:26 - NKJV**), He was initiating more than a creative act—He was unveiling a project of cosmic intimacy. Humanity was not created to be servants in a distant empire, but sons and daughters in the household of God. We were not formed as clergy or religious elites, but as co-creators, co-rulers, and stewards of a living universe infused with divine breath.

This is humanity's true beginning, not in fear, but in fellowship; not as exiles, but as those entrusted with divine dominion.

"Then God said, 'Let Us make man in Our image, according to Our likeness; let them have dominion...'" (Genesis 1:26–27 - NKJV).

God's intention was not merely to walk with man, but to dwell in man, to share life at the deepest level of being. Eden was more than a garden; it was a prototype, a portal, the original interface where heaven kissed earth. It was a place of intimacy where God and man cohabited in undivided harmony.

Mystic and theologian Gregory of Nyssa taught that *"the goal of the virtuous life is to become like God."* In Eden, that likeness was not a future goal, it was a present reality. We didn't simply carry God's image as a label; we embodied it as a living expression of divine essence.

THE FALL WAS ONTOLOGICAL, NOT MERELY MORAL

Humanity's fall was not simply the violation of a rule, it was a rupture of reality. We didn't just disobey; we disintegrated. We became disconnected from our Source, and in doing so, lost the capacity to function as intended. As Thomas Merton reflected, *"Sin is the refusal to become who we truly are."*

We were created to radiate glory, not survive in shame. The fall shattered that capacity, not because God revoked it, but because we abandoned it.

"For all have sinned and fall short of the glory of God." (Romans 3:23 - NKJV).

The word "glory" (doxa) is not just moral uprightness, it refers to weight, radiance, and divine splendor. We lost the capacity to carry glory, and thus fell into a cycle of survival, hiding, and striving. That is the bad news.

The good news is that in Christ, the union is restored.

"For God was in Christ, reconciling the world to Himself, no longer counting people's sins against them..." (2 Corinthians 5:19 - NLT).

The restoration is not merely legal, it is ontological. We are made new, not just in status but in substance.

"...put on the new man who is renewed in knowledge according to the image of Him who created him." (Colossians 3:10 - NKJV).

In Christ, we are not escaping hell. We are re-entering Eden. This is not a literal place, but a mystical posture—a restored union with God.

THE IMPORTANCE OF FOCUS: FROM EARTH TO ETERNITY

Paul's instructions are both practical and mystical:

"Set your mind on things above, not on things on the earth." (Colossians 3:2 - NKJV).

Why? Because what we focus on, we become aligned with. When we live consumed by the temporal, we forfeit the eternal. The world we see is not the most real—it is the most temporary.

"For the things which are seen are temporary, but the things which are not seen are eternal." (2 Corinthians 4:18 - NKJV).

As Meister Eckhart taught, *"The eye with which I see God is the same eye with which God sees me."* This points to contemplative awareness—a return to the kind of consciousness that was once natural in Eden.

Christianity, rightly understood, is not a strategy for escape from a doomed earth, but the transformation of the world through transformed beings. We are not raptured from creation; we are redeemed within it—as first fruits of a new creation.

"So if anyone is in Christ [that is, grafted in, joined to Him by faith], he is a new creature [reborn and renewed by the Holy Spirit]; the old things [the previous moral and spiritual condition] have passed away." (2 Corinthians 5:17 - AMP).

JESUS' PRAYER: NOT ESCAPE, BUT ENGAGEMENT

In His final prayer, Jesus says something striking:

"I do not pray that You should take them out of the world, but that You should keep them from the evil one." (John 17:15 - NKJV).

Jesus wasn't forming an escapist theology. He was preparing a people who could carry divine presence into the darkness. As St. Teresa of Ávila famously said, *"Christ has no body now but yours."* We are His interface—His Edenic temple—in the midst of a groaning creation.

THE BOOK OF JOB: A GLIMPSE OF PRE-FALL CAPACITY?

In reflecting on our original mandate, I found myself drawn to the book of Job. Although it appears late in the Bible, it is likely the oldest book, set long before Moses and Abraham. Why then, is it placed so far back in the canon? Perhaps because it contains ancient wisdom we have yet to fully grasp.

When God finally speaks to Job, He unleashes a torrent of questions—questions not of condemnation, but revelation. In Job 38–41, God challenges Job: **"Can you command the morning, and cause the dawn to know its place?" (Job 38:12 - NKJV). "Can you bind the cluster of the Pleiades, or loose the belt of Orion?" (Job 38:31 - NKJV).**

These are strange questions often interpreted as rhetorical reminders of divine supremacy. But what if they also hint at original human capacity—what we were once capable of in union with God before we fell?

What if man, in his pre-fallen form, was designed not merely to observe nature, but to partner with it—to influence weather, tend the elements, commune with animals, and steward energy? Is it possible that Adam could do in the

Garden what Jesus did on the sea—speak to storms and silence them?

"What manner of man is this, that even the wind and the sea obey Him!" (Mark 4:41 - NKJV).

Jesus, the Second Adam, wasn't displaying divine showmanship—He was revealing restored humanity.

THE JOURNEY BACK HAS BEGUN

If there is even the slightest possibility that Job's dialogue with God reflects man's lost function, then the restoration of God's original mandate has already begun in Christ. The "Yes" we speak in faith is not just assent to salvation, it is alignment with our ancient assignment.

We were created to govern, not dominate; to cultivate, not exploit; to embody heaven, not escape earth.

"The creation waits in eager expectation for the sons of God to be revealed." (Romans 8:19 - NKJV).

And that revelation begins the moment we say yes to Christ. The image of God is restored, not just for heaven someday, but for the earth right now. You are not a church member waiting to die and go to heaven. You are a divine agent reborn to reimagine the world in union with the One who created it.

Eden is not lost, it is within reach.

Initially, I wanted this book to be semi-academic in nature. I am a seminary student after all. But I still prefer clear and simple communication when it comes to theological reflections because I want to appeal to the younger generation.

Just in case the academic tone is too much to process, I want to simplify the concepts so far. As a human being, you are no ordinary creation. If you are born again, you are even more extra-ordinary. The mandate given to humanity is not purely a spiritual one in the ethereal realm as Christians often desire and speak about. You were created as a physical being to govern a physical creation. So the mandate then is still the same today. Our goal and eventual destination is a new heaven and a new earth in a physical, glorified body. If you really think about it, my presupposition is that we will be like Adam before the fall in form and function: a glorified, resurrected, redeemed body is the original created by God when He said, **"Let Us make man in Our image and likeness…"**

Jesus is the first since Adam to walk in one such body. We will follow. Our reign will be on a new earth in a physical body, not a spiritual form. This is where we are going, which means it becomes our reality now—the already-but-not-yet because we still exist in time.

Let the journey continue.

Chapter 6

The World Jesus Entered

"But when the fullness of the time had come, God sent forth His Son, born of a woman, born under the law." (Galatians 4:4 - NKJV).

Jesus did not descend into a vacuum of silence or spiritual apathy; He entered a world charged with longing, divided by systems, weighed down by oppression, and aching for redemption. The incarnation happened not in tranquillity, but in a collision of competing kingdoms, fractured religious ideologies, and deeply unmet expectations. To grasp the radical nature of Jesus' mission, we must first understand the world He came into.

Though the Old Testament closes with the book of Malachi, the so-called "400 years of silence" between Malachi and Matthew were anything but still. These centuries were rich with conflict, apocalyptic fervor, and escalating disillusionment. God may not have spoken through a recognized prophet in that time, but humanity was shouting into the heavens, craving divine response.

A WORLD ON THE EDGE

Religious factions emerged to fill the prophetic silence. Each had a vision for restoring Israel's glory, yet each missed the heart of the Father:

- ☙ The Pharisees elevated oral tradition and legalistic purity, believing strict adherence to the Law would usher in God's favor.

- ☙ The Sadducees, aligned with Roman political power, denied the supernatural and controlled temple worship for profit and prestige.

- ☙ The Essenes, disgusted by corruption, retreated into desert monasticism and awaited an apocalyptic deliverer.

- ☙ The Zealots pursued violent revolution, convinced that overthrowing Rome would restore the kingdom.

Amid these factions, a growing Hellenistic influence (thanks to Alexander the Great) introduced a wave of Greek philosophy, rationalism, and secularism. The Jewish world became increasingly conflicted between its sacred traditions and the allure of intellectual sophistication. The stage was set for something radical, yet almost no one recognized the divine entrance when it happened.

This was the fullness of time; a time saturated with messianic expectation, yet utterly unprepared for the kind of Messiah God would send.

"He came to His own, and His own did not receive Him." (John 1:11 - NKJV).

THE PAX ROMANA AND THE POLITICS OF OPPRESSION

Rome's so-called "Pax Romana" was not peace as heaven defines it. It was peace through the suppression of dissent, a fragile stability enforced by brutality. Crucifixion, heavy taxation, and emperor worship were standard tools of the empire. Caesar was hailed as "Lord" and "son of God"—a blasphemous counterfeit to the true Son who would soon be born in Bethlehem.

Jesus entered into this world of imperial propaganda, not to start a competing religion, but to announce a kingdom "**not of this world**" (see John 18:36). His arrival wasn't a diplomatic gesture; it was a divine invasion.

GOD AMONG US, BUT UNRECOGNIZED

The most haunting indictment of Jesus' ministry was that the most religious people of His day missed Him entirely.

"You search the Scriptures, for in them you think you have eternal life; and these are they which testify of Me. But you are not willing to come to Me..." (John 5:39–40 - NKJV).

This wasn't ignorance, it was inversion. They had mastered the letter but missed the Spirit. The scribes could quote Isaiah yet had no ears for Isaiah's God. They recited the Psalms but could not recognize the Shepherd. As Richard Rohr often writes, *"The problem is that religion often teaches us what to see, but not how to see."*

Their understanding of God had become so systematized that when God appeared in flesh, He was seen as a threat.

LONGINGS FOUND IN APOCRYPHAL WRITINGS

During this same era, extra-biblical writings like The Book of Enoch, 4 Ezra, and fragments from the Dead Sea Scrolls testify to the deep mystical and apocalyptic consciousness of the time:

- ∝ A longing for supernatural intervention.

- ∝ Belief in angelic hierarchies and cosmic battles.

- ∝ A fear that the religious leadership was corrupted beyond repair.

- ∝ An expectation that two messiahs would come: one priestly, one kingly.

Though not canonical, these texts mirror the psychic and spiritual tension in Jewish culture. The people wanted God to come, but not like this. They wanted a warrior. They got a carpenter. They wanted thrones. They got a cross.

"For He shall grow up before Him as a tender plant, and as a root out of dry ground. He has no form or comeliness; And when we see Him, there is no beauty that we should desire Him. He is despised and rejected by

men, a Man of sorrows and acquainted with grief. And we hid, as it were, our faces from Him; He was despised, and we did not esteem Him." (Isaiah 53:2–3 - NKJV).

HE CAME TO END RELIGION, NOT REINFORCE IT

When Jesus came, He didn't offer a new belief system; He offered a new creation. He didn't heal to prove a point. He healed to restore original design. Every miracle was a signpost pointing back to Eden and forward to the kingdom.

"Destroy this temple, and in three days I will raise it up." (John 2:19 - NKJV).

They thought He spoke of bricks and mortar. He was speaking of Himself: the new dwelling place of God among men. He didn't come to renovate the religious system; He came to replace it with Himself. As Paul would later write: **"For there is one God and one Mediator between God and men, the Man Christ Jesus." (1 Timothy 2:5 - NKJV).**

The mystic Evelyn Underhill once noted that religion often serves as *"a veil too thick for the light it tries to transmit."* Jesus came to tear the veil, not with gradual reform, but with divine disruption.

"And the veil of the temple was torn in two from top to bottom." (Mark 15:38 - AMP).

The dividing line between God and man was not softened—it was shattered.

WOULD WE RECOGNIZE HIM TODAY?

Christianity was born in a world where religion had become an idol and God had become unrecognizable. Jesus came not to add another stream to the religious river, but to reroute it back to the source: to reclaim humanity from its fragmentation.

If Jesus walked among us today, would the churches built in His name recognize Him? Or would we be offended by His methods, His message, His lack of decorum?

Would we be like the Pharisees who asked, *"By what authority do You do these things?"* Or would we hear the still small voice in the carpenter from Nazareth?

"He was in the world, and the world was made through Him, and the world did not know Him." (John 1:10 - NKJV).

It is a sad reality that we can be so blinded by our own ideologies that we miss God. The sobering truth is: *Jesus may be more offensive to religious structures now than He was then.* Our systems, like theirs, love control more than union; appearances more than transformation.

Jesus didn't come to improve our systems. He came to become the system. Christianity was never meant to be a religion to practice but the person of Christ to encounter.

Chapter 7

Born Again—Divine Metamorphosis

To be born again is not simply a moral upgrade or a new belief system—it is a metaphysical rupture. It is not a self-improvement project; it is a self-surrendered exchange. As Paul boldly declares: **"I have been crucified with Christ; it is no longer I who live, but Christ lives in me…"** (Galatians 2:20 - NKJV).

The old self is not rehabilitated, it is put to death. What rises in its place is not a slightly better version of what was, but an entirely new creation: a being birthed from the eternal, drawn from the divine DNA of God Himself.

"Jesus answered him, 'I assure you and most solemnly say to you, unless a person is born again [reborn from

above—spiritually transformed, renewed, sanctified], he cannot [ever] see and experience the kingdom of God.'" (John 3:3 - AMP).

This is not metaphor. This is transformation at the level of essence. The mystics knew this well. Meister Eckhart once said, *"God is at home, it is we who have gone out for a walk."* Being born again is not about finding a new direction; it's about returning home to our true origin—God.

THE RETURN OF THE BREATH

At the moment of rebirth, something primordial is restored: the breath of God re-enters the dust of humanity. This echoes the very beginning, when God formed Adam and **"breathed into his nostrils the breath of life"** (see Genesis 2:7). In Christ, that same breath—divine Spirit— reanimates us.

"But if the Spirit of Him who raised Jesus from the dead dwells in you, He who raised Christ... will also give life to your mortal bodies through His Spirit who dwells in you." (Romans 8:11 - NKJV).

The soul, once fragmented and dormant, is quickened. The spirit, once alienated, is reunited with Source. The body, though still susceptible to death, becomes a living temple, charged with eternal presence: **"Do you not know that your body is the temple of the Holy Spirit who is in you… and you are not your own?" (1 Corinthians 6:19 - NKJV).**

This is not a mere legal declaration of righteousness, it is the reigniting of divine design.

FROM UNION FLOWS IDENTITY

We are not merely saved from something, we are reborn into someone. Union with Christ is not the reward of a good life; it is the foundation of the new life.

"It's in Christ that we find out who we are and what we are living for." (Ephesians 1:11 - MSG).

This union is not symbolic, it is organic. The same Spirit that raised Jesus from the grave now indwells us. We are grafted into divine life. This is what Paul calls: **"Christ in you, the hope of glory." (Colossians 1:27 - NKJV).**

Christianity is not about sin management. It is about identity metamorphosis. The mystic Madame Jeanne Guyon wrote, *"The soul's union with God begins with the knowledge of who God is but deepens when we understand who we are in Him."*

To be born again is to become one with the Christ-nature, not just in theory, but in lived embodiment.

PARTICIPATION IN CHRIST'S JOURNEY

When we say "yes" to Christ, we are not joining a religion, we are entering a cosmic sequence. We are mystically joined to His life, His death, His burial, His resurrection, and His ascension. This is not symbolic language. It is the mystery Paul proclaims: **"Even when we were dead in trespasses, [God] made us alive together with Christ... and raised us up together, and made us sit together in the heavenly places in Christ Jesus." (Ephesians 2:5–6 - NKJV).**

We are not waiting to go to heaven someday—we are already seated in it, spiritually aligned with Christ's victory and authority. As Watchman Nee once described in The Normal Christian Life, we move from *"Christian experience"* to *"Christian position."* We don't strive to reach glory; we begin from it.

REGENESIS: THE RESTORATION OF THE IMAGE

To be born again is to be restored to Edenic intent. God is not patching up fallen humanity, He is creating something entirely new. The second birth is the reinstatement of Imago Dei—God's image and likeness reawakened in us.

"He predestined us to be conformed to the image of His Son…" (Romans 8:29 - NKJV).

This is not philosophical, it is ontological. The new birth changes what we are, not just how we behave. Theologian Karl Rahner once said, *"The Christian of the future will be a mystic or he will not exist at all."* This is precisely because Christianity, at its core, is about becoming one with God.

To be born again is not to receive a new belief system, it is to receive a new being.

"Therefore, if anyone is in Christ [that is, grafted in, joined to Him by faith], he is a new creature [reborn and renewed by the Holy Spirit]; the old things have passed away." (2 Corinthians 5:17 - AMP).

And this new creature is not ordinary.

THE NEW CREATION IS NOT A BETTER VERSION, IT IS A DIVINE BEING

The one who is in Christ is not a repaired version of the fallen self. The new creation is of a different order, a different species, so to speak. The Greek word for "new" (kainos) in 2 Corinthians 5:17 implies something unprecedented, never seen before.

We are not human beings trying to behave divinely. We are divine beings clothed in humanity, called to reveal heaven on earth. As mystic and poet Thomas Traherne wrote, *"You never enjoy the world aright, till the sea itself floweth in your veins."*

DIVINE METAMORPHOSIS HAS BEGUN

The journey of the soul is not linear, it is spiral. As we grow in awareness of who we are in Christ, we begin to live from that identity rather than striving toward it.

"And all of us… are being transformed into His image with ever-increasing glory." (2 Corinthians 3:18 - AMP).

To be born again is to begin this unfolding metamorphosis, one that begins in spirit and reaches toward wholeness: body, soul, and mind. It is not the culmination of our journey; it is the portal into the life we were always meant to live.

This is divine metamorphosis. This is the mystery of new birth. This is the New Creation Code being activated in you.

Chapter 8

Theosis Without Idolatry

The idea that God dwells in human beings has always been both breathtaking and controversial. It is the mystery of incarnation extended. Christ did not only enter human flesh in history, but He now inhabits human lives in the present. To believe that the eternal can dwell in the temporal, that the infinite can be joined with the finite, is to step into the mystery of Theosis.

But this union, glorious as it is, must be approached with awe and precision. We are walking on sacred ground. To speak of becoming **"partakers of the divine nature"** (see 2 Peter 1:4) is not to blur the boundary between Creator and creation, but to honor the mystery of divine participation without confusion.

"For by these He has bestowed on us His precious and magnificent promises... so that by them you may escape from the immoral freedom that is in the world... and become sharers of the divine nature." (2 Peter 1:4 - AMP).

PARTICIPATION, NOT POSSESSION

The early church Fathers held this mystery in tension. Athanasius, a fourth-century bishop and defender of Nicene orthodoxy, famously declared: *"God became man so that man might become god."*

This was not a reckless statement. It was a theological anchor. Athanasius wasn't advocating self-deification, but a graced transformation through union with Christ. We do not become God by essence or nature—we are not absorbed into the divine—but we are invited to participate in His life by grace.

We are not the light itself—we are bearers of it. We are not the source—we are vessels. We are not rivals—we are reflections.

As Paul wrote, **"But we have this treasure in earthen vessels, that the excellence of the power may be of God and not of us."** (2 Corinthians 4:7 - NKJV).

TEMPLES, NOT ARCHITECTS

To experience Theosis is to be animated by the life of God, not elevated to His throne. We become temples of the Holy Spirit (see 1 Corinthians 6:19), but we are not the architects of our own holiness. We do not initiate divinity; we host it. This participation humbles us rather than exalts us.

"Or do you not know that your body is a temple of the Holy Spirit who is within you... and that you are not your own?" (1 Corinthians 6:19 - AMP).

The mystic St. John of the Cross echoed this beautifully: *"The soul that is in love with God is transformed into God, not by nature, but by participation."*

The more we are filled with God, the less of ourselves remains in the selfish sense. True union dissolves the ego, not inflates it.

To say **"Christ lives in me"** (see Galatians 2:20) is not a declaration of spiritual superiority, but of surrendered identity. It is the paradox of divine life: we become most like God when we are least preoccupied with ourselves.

"The life you see me living is not 'mine,' but it is lived by faith in the Son of God, who loved me and gave himself for me." (Galatians 2:20 - MSG).

GUARDING THE MYSTERY: NO ROOM FOR GNOSTICISM OR NEW AGE CONFUSION

In our time, the language of union has been co-opted by spiritual counterfeits—New Age movements, Gnostic reinterpretations, and pseudo-mystical frameworks that promote the idea of divinity as self-originating. But biblical Theosis is rooted not in personal enlightenment, but in Christic union.

We do not awaken to our inner god-self. We are reborn into divine life through Christ alone.

Jesus is not merely a model to emulate—He is the very source and sustainer of the new creation life within us.

"Remain in Me, and I will remain in you. Just as no branch can bear fruit by itself... neither can you bear fruit unless you remain in Me." (John 15:4 - AMP).

WE ARE DEFINED BY WHAT WE CONTAIN

We are vessels—containers of divine life. As such, our worth is not in the material of our clay, but in the glory we carry.

"Don't you realize that you are the temple of God, and that God himself is present in you?" (1 Corinthians 3:16 - MSG).

Mystics throughout history have wrestled with this holy tension. Julian of Norwich declared, *"God is nearer to us than our own soul."* Yet she never confused that nearness with sameness. The vessel is not the treasure, but the vessel, when yielded, reveals the treasure.

THE MYSTERY IN OUR BLOOD

Scripture says, **"The life of the flesh is in the blood..."** (Leviticus 17:11 - NKJV).

Modern science, when observing human blood at the quantum level, finds that it reflects light—plasma-like in nature. Some mystics and theologians have postulated that this "light" is an echo of our original glory. While we must not build doctrine on speculation, it is consistent with the biblical theme that humanity was designed to carry divine radiance.

We were created not in sin, but in glory. Sin is not our origin, it is the distortion. Redemption is not just forgiveness; it is the restoration of what was glorious and radiant from the beginning.

"Arise, shine; for your light has come! And the glory of the Lord is risen upon you." (Isaiah 60:1 - NKJV).

UNION WITHOUT IDOLATRY

The more we grow in union with God, the more we must guard against the temptation to exalt ourselves or our creations. Anything we create that is separated from God's presence, or which seeks to replace God, becomes an idol.

"You shall have no other gods before Me." (Exodus 20:3 - NKJV).

Even spiritual language can become an idol if it disconnects us from dependence on God. Theosis does not mean autonomy. It means absolute dependence, grounded in divine intimacy.

As Thomas Merton observed: *"A humble man is not afraid of being forgotten, because he knows he is remembered by God."*

THE CALL TO PARTICIPATE, NOT SPECTATE

God is not calling us to admire what He is doing in creation. He is calling us to participate in it. Union leads to mission, not as effort, but as overflow. We carry the presence, not to display power, but to reveal love.

"For we are co-workers in God's service; you are God's field, God's building." (1 Corinthians 3:9 - NIV).

To be one with God is not to become independent, but to be radically intertwined—a branch drawing its life from the Vine, a temple filled with fire, a soul made luminous with grace.

IN SUMMARY

- ⟨ℬ⟩ Theosis is not self-deification; it is grace-formed participation in divine life.

- ⟨ℬ⟩ We do not become God, but we are made like Him through union.

- ⟨ℬ⟩ True union leads to humility, not pride.

- ⟨ℬ⟩ We are temples, not architects; vessels, not sources.

- ⟨ℬ⟩ Any identity apart from divine union devolves into idolatry.

- ⟨ℬ⟩ God calls us not to spectate from a distance but to participate in His life—from within.

This is the mystery of godliness: Christ in you, the hope of glory.

Chapter 9

Christianity Is Not...

To understand what Christianity truly is, we must first confront what it is not.

Much of what passes as Christianity today is a diluted, distorted, and domesticated version of its original power—a hollowed-out form that preserves the name of Jesus while denying the fire of His presence. The early followers of Christ did not consider themselves part of a "religion." They were members of The Way (see Acts 9:2)—a way of being, of living, and of union with God through Christ.

"I am the Way, the Truth, and the Life. No one comes to the Father except through Me." (John 14:6 - NKJV).

The Way was not a creed to recite but a path to walk. It was not institutional; it was incarnational. Christianity, in its original form, was the divine life expressed in human vessels; it was not meant to be a religion to be observed but a mystery to be entered.

As the mystic Evelyn Underhill once said, *"The spiritual life is not a special career, but a destiny for every person. It is not taught by rote but caught by fire."*

CHRISTIANITY IS NOT RELIGION

Religion is humanity's attempt to climb toward God through structure, law, and performance. Christianity is God's descent into humanity—God reaching for us through the incarnation of Christ.

"For the law was given through Moses, but grace and truth came through Jesus Christ." (John 1:17 - NKJV).

Religion binds us to rituals. Grace binds us to God.

Jesus did not come to establish another religious system. He came to render religion obsolete. The veil in the temple tore at His death for a reason: **"Then, behold, the veil of the temple was torn in two from top to bottom..." (Matthew 27:51 - NKJV).**

God was no longer confined to buildings, priests, or rituals. Access to the Father was fully opened—direct, personal, and unending.

"And so, dear brothers and sisters, we can now boldly enter heaven's Most Holy Place because of the blood of Jesus." (Hebrews 10:19 - NLT).

Christianity, then, is not about approaching God through religion, but about the indwelling of God through union.

CHRISTIANITY IS NOT LAW-BASED

The law regulates behavior from the outside. Grace transforms identity from the inside. The law says: *"Do this and live."* Grace says: *"Live—and you will do this."*

As Paul writes: **"Clearly, you are a letter from Christ... not written with pen and ink, but with the Spirit of the living God. It is carved not on tablets of stone, but on human hearts." (2 Corinthians 3:3 - NLT).**

Commandments written on stone can inform, but only Spirit-written truth on the heart can transform. Mystic teacher Thomas à Kempis put it simply: *"External actions are meaningless unless they flow from inward union with Christ."*

CHRISTIANITY IS NOT WORK-BASED

You cannot earn God's love. You cannot impress God with performance. Salvation is not a wage—it is a gift.

"For by grace you have been saved through faith, and that not of yourselves; it is the gift of God, not of works..." (Ephesians 2:8–9 - NKJV).

No amount of church attendance, volunteer hours, or moral behavior can substitute for the miracle of rebirth. You are not a better version of your old self. You are new.

"Jesus answered... 'Unless one is born again, he cannot see the kingdom of God.'" (John 3:3 - NKJV).

What disqualifies us is not primarily our behavior, but our lineage. We were born into a fallen race. The solution is not rehabilitation, but regeneration.

"When God our Savior revealed His kindness and love, He saved us, not because of the righteous things we had done, but because of His mercy. He washed away our sins, giving us a new birth and new life through the Holy Spirit." (Titus 3:4–5 - NLT).

CHRISTIANITY IS NOT MORALISM

Christianity is not a behavior code. It is a life exchanged.

Morality can restrain the flesh, but it cannot resurrect the spirit. The fruit of the Spirit does not grow from human willpower—it flows from abiding in divine presence.

"But the fruit of the Spirit is love, joy, peace, longsuffering, kindness, goodness, faithfulness…" **(Galatians 5:22–23 - NKJV).**

Jesus did not die to make bad people good. He came to make dead people alive.

"And you He made alive, who were dead in trespasses and sins." (Ephesians 2:1 - NKJV).

As Richard Rohr often says, *"The opposite of sin is not virtue. The opposite of sin is union."* Christianity doesn't just change your habits; it changes your nature.

CHRISTIANITY IS NOT CULTURAL CONFORMITY

True Christianity does not conform to culture—it transforms it.

Jesus didn't fit into the religious or political systems of His day. He disrupted them. He touched lepers, embraced Samaritans, confronted Pharisees, and elevated women. His gospel was dangerously inclusive and relentlessly counter-cultural.

"Don't become so well-adjusted to your culture that you fit into it without even thinking." (Romans 12:2 - MSG).

If your version of Christianity requires cultural approval, it's not Christianity—it's idolatry.

As A.W. Tozer warned, *"The church that cannot endure rejection by the world is not the church of Jesus Christ."*

CHRISTIANITY IS NOT SAFE, TAME, OR ENTERTAINMENT-DRIVEN

One of the greatest dangers in our time is not overt rebellion against God, but a domesticated Christianity—a Jesus who comforts but never convicts, who affirms but never transforms.

This false gospel entertains but does not awaken. It builds empires, but forfeits intimacy. It offers inspiration, but not incarnation.

As the Spirit said through Paul: **"Having a form of godliness but denying its power…"** (2 Timothy 3:5 - NKJV).

This is not true Christianity. This is the shell without the Spirit, the ritual without the fire, the name without the nature.

IN SUMMARY

- 03 Christianity is union with Christ, not affiliation with a system.

- 03 It is Spirit and truth, not law and performance.

- 03 It is the indwelling of God, not a belief about God.

- 03 It is transformation, not modification.

- 03 It is a new creation, not a better routine.

To follow Jesus is not to join a religion. It is to awaken to the divine life within you, and to walk in the Way, empowered by the Spirit, rooted in love, and ablaze with glory.

That—and only that—is true Christianity.

Chapter 10

Real Christianity

"Do not be conformed to this world, but be transformed by the renewing of your mind..." (Romans 12:2 - NKJV).

The Christian life is not defined by intellectual assent or moral restraint, it is the journey of transformation. Paul's call is clear: we are not to fit into the mold of a broken world system, but to be remade by a renewed mind, shaped not by culture or tradition, but by the living reality of Christ within.

Real Christianity is not passive, it is participatory. It is not about joining an institution but entering into the ongoing mission of God. It is not simply receiving salvation; it is becoming salvation's expression in a groaning world.

The mystic and theologian St. Maximus the Confessor wrote, *"The Word of God, who wills that all should be saved and come to the knowledge of the truth, goes forth to find those who are lost, and He makes them shepherds of others."*

Christianity is the redeemed becoming the redeemer. We do not save in our own name, but we carry the One who saves in His.

"As the Father has sent Me, I also send you." (John 20:21 - NKJV).

"All this is from God, who reconciled us to Himself through Christ and gave us the ministry of reconciliation." (2 Corinthians 5:18 - AMP).

REDEEMED TO REDEEM

Redemption is not the end of the Christian story, it is the beginning. We are not just saved from sin, but for purpose. We do not simply receive the work of Christ, we become participants in it.

The goal is not simply to be delivered, but to become deliverers. This is not a shift in identity, but the fulfilment of identity. As we are united with Christ, His mission becomes ours.

The 14th-century mystic John Ruysbroeck spoke of this divine exchange when he wrote, *"God being mine and I His, all things become possible, and the world is transformed by our love."*

THE FORGIVEN BECOMING THE FORGIVER

Jesus made forgiveness central, not only as a gift received, but as a reality reproduced.

"Forgive us our debts, as we forgive our debtors." (Matthew 6:12 - NKJV).

We forgive, not because we are commanded to but because we have been so radically forgiven that it becomes natural. Forgiveness flows not from obligation but from overflow.

"Be kind to one another, tenderhearted, forgiving one another, just as God in Christ forgave you." (Ephesians 4:32 - NKJV).

True forgiveness is not a transaction, it is transformation. It frees the forgiver as much as the forgiven. In forgiving, we participate in the healing of the world.

THE DELIVERED BECOMING THE DELIVERER

"These signs will follow those who believe: In My name they will cast out demons..." (Mark 16:17 - NKJV).

Jesus not only delivered the oppressed, He authorized His followers to do the same. Deliverance is not a fringe ministry. It is the fruit of authority flowing from union.

We are not just rescued victims, we are now agents of liberation. As Jesus said in Luke 4, He came to proclaim liberty to the captives. Now He proclaims it through us.

"He called His twelve disciples together and gave them power and authority over all demons, and to cure diseases." (Luke 9:1 - NKJV).

THE HEALED BECOMING THE HEALER

"By His stripes we are healed." (Isaiah 53:5 - NKJV).

Jesus did not simply heal to display power, He healed to reveal the Father's compassion. He then commissioned His followers to do the same.

"He sent them out to proclaim the kingdom of God and to heal the sick." (Luke 9:2 - MSG).

Healing is not performance, it is participation in the divine compassion and wholeness that flows from the indwelling Spirit.

"And these signs will accompany those who believe... they will lay hands on the sick, and they will recover." (Mark 16:17–18 - AMP).

THE RESTORED BECOMING THE RESTORER

"But now in Christ Jesus you who once were far off have been brought near by the blood of Christ." (Ephesians 2:13 - NKJV).

Restoration is not a private luxury, it is a public responsibility. Those who have been made whole are called to rebuild what has been broken.

"Your people will rebuild the ancient ruins and will raise up the age-old foundations; you will be called Repairer of the Breach." (Isaiah 58:12 - AMP).

We are not here to escape the world, we are here to restore it, one soul, one home, one community at a time. Every act of kindness, every stand for justice, every word of truth becomes an act of spiritual construction.

THE LOVED BECOMING THE LOVER

"We love Him because He first loved us." (1 John 4:19 - NKJV).

Love is not the conclusion of Christianity; it is the foundation. Without love, all prophetic insight and spiritual gifting is void of value (see 1 Corinthians 13:1–3).

"Let me give you a new command: Love one another. In the same way I loved you, you love one another." (John 13:34 - MSG).

Jesus didn't tell us to be right. He told us to be love. Love is not weak. It is the strongest spiritual technology in the universe. Love doesn't merely affirm, it transforms. Love heals, restores, and sets the atmosphere for miracles.

"The entire law is fulfilled in keeping this one command: 'Love your neighbor as yourself.'" (Galatians 5:14 - NIV).

Mystics like St. Catherine of Siena insisted that *"All the way to heaven is heaven, because Christ is the Way."* That way is always the way of love.

PARTICIPATION, NOT PERFORMANCE

Real Christianity is not a spectator event. It is a living union, a sacred participation in the ongoing mission of Christ.

We do not hoard what we have received—we become it. We do not merely admire Jesus—we embody His mission. We do not wait for change—we become the change.

"It is no longer I who live, but Christ lives in me..." (Galatians 2:20 - NKJV).

"Anyone who intends to come with Me has to let Me lead. You're not in the driver's seat—I am." (Luke 9:23 - MSG).

REAL CHRISTIANITY IS...

ↄ The redeemed becoming redeemers.

ↄ The forgiven becoming forgivers.

ↄ The healed becoming healers.

ↄ The delivered becoming deliverers.

ↄ The restored becoming restorers.

ᴄꜱ The loved becoming lovers.

It is not about power for self, but power through surrender. It is not about performing for God but participating with Him.

Real Christianity is Christ continuing His life through ours.

Chapter 11

Overcoming the World

Christianity is about overcoming.

There are several mentions of the rewards reserved for overcomers in the Book of Revelation. In fact, to each of the seven churches, Christ's final word is the same: **"To the one who overcomes…" (Revelation 2–3).** This overcoming is not optional, it is central to the identity of the believer in Christ. The message is consistent: *we are not merely saved to survive but to overcome.*

Too often on our journey of faith, our proclivities to the fallen nature are sometimes embraced as normal. This should not be.

Jesus says in John 16:33: **"I have told you these things, so that in Me you may have [perfect] peace. In the world** you have tribulation and distress and suffering, but be courageous [be confident, be undaunted, be filled with joy]; I have overcome the world. [My conquest is accomplished, My victory abiding.]" (AMP).

His overcoming is our pattern. His victory is our inheritance.

There are things within our fallen nature that must be overcome and transmuted. This applies to every believer. Coming into the faith doesn't fix our problems or make us immune to the things we struggled with prior. It simply sets us on a path to face our issues with truth, surrender, and spiritual power—and to overcome them through union with Christ.

Teresa of Ávila, a great Christian mystic, once said: *"The soul is like a castle made of a single diamond… and in this castle are many rooms, just as in Heaven there are many mansions. But most souls live in the outer courtyard and never enter within."*

The implication is clear: transformation is a journey inward. Overcoming is the movement from the fragmented self to the whole, Christ-formed self.

I have observed the struggle of homosexuality within my own church denomination. I realize that this practice is embraced and even thought to be a natural genetic predisposition. In other words, one is born a homosexual and to fight it is like going to war with one's true self. But as mentioned earlier, no one can sin without first believing a lie.

To be clear, the issue here is not limited to any single struggle. For some, the struggle is fornication, lust, adultery, lying. We all have something we struggle with that must be overcome. This is the universal reality of fallen humanity, and the common battleground of spiritual maturity.

I have learned from my own experience that overcoming is much more than just making a decision not to do something. It is not behavior management. It is death and resurrection.

Paul says: **"For what I am doing, I do not understand. For what I will to do, that I do not practice; but what I hate, that I do." (Romans 7:15 - NKJV). "O wretched man that I am! Who will deliver me from this body of death? I thank God—through Jesus Christ our Lord!" (Romans 7:24–25 - NKJV).**

He ends that whole poetic discourse with the cry, **"Who will deliver me from this body of death?"** The answer is Christ, and the path is death to the false self.

He continues in 1 Corinthians 15:31: **"I die daily."**

The principle of overcoming is death to that 'us' that feels like us but is not us. The mystics referred to this false self as the old man, the mask of ego, the self that lives in separation from God. We must never accept any concept, ideology, personality or character that is rooted in the fallen nature of man because it is not our true nature. We must contend with both—the false and the true. To embrace the former is to embrace something false about ourselves as if it were truth.

Meister Eckhart put it bluntly: *"God is not found in the soul by adding anything but by a process of subtraction."*

This leads us to act contrary to our true nature and indulge in sinful activities. Sin is essentially doing what is not-God.

There are too many Christians who have not overcome their natural proclivities, so they choose instead to live a fragmented life. This is why today we have an abomination called a Christian gay pastor.

Never accept sin as a normal genetic disposition.

Julian of Norwich reminds us: *"Sin is behovely (necessary), but all shall be well, and all shall be well, and all manner of thing shall be well."*

Her mystical vision was not one of permissiveness but one of hope. Sin is a reality we contend with, but its power is not final. We are not defined by our desires but by our destiny in Christ.

The ancients are right when they said our greatest enemy is not without but within. In overcoming that which is embedded within, any force outside us will lose its foothold and influence.

As Jesus said: **"For the ruler of this world is coming, and he has nothing in Me." (John 14:30 - NKJV).**

He had no agreement with the darkness, no uncrucified desire, no hidden allegiance. That is the calling of the overcomer: to be so unified with Christ that the enemy finds nothing in us to manipulate.

When you overcome, you help others to overcome. Your victory becomes their permission.

Revelation 12:11 declares: **"They defeated him through the blood of the Lamb and the bold word of their witness. They weren't in love with themselves; they were willing to die for Christ."** (MSG).

Overcoming is costly but it produces the fragrance of Christ and it sets captives free.

In contending with fallen beings, the first Adam failed. The second Adam did not, proving that it is possible to overcome the issues that seek to control and skew our true identity.

To this Paul says: **"For as in Adam all die, even so in Christ all shall be made alive."** (1 Corinthians 15:22 - NKJV).

"Therefore, if anyone is in Christ, he is a new creation; old things have passed away; behold, all things have become new." (2 Corinthians 5:17 - NKJV).

It is not merely forgiveness we receive, it is transformation.

Theologian and mystic Evelyn Underhill wrote: *"The spiritual life is not a special career, involving abstraction from the world of things, but the normal development of humanity. The mystic is not a special kind of person; every person is a special kind of mystic."*

Overcoming is not reserved for a few but required of all. It is the very trajectory of salvation—from justification to sanctification to glorification. It is becoming who we truly are in Christ and putting to death everything in us that resists that truth.

So what must we do? We yield. We surrender. We die daily. We recognize that Christ has already overcome, and we live from that victory. As the Apostle John reminds us: **"For whatever is born of God overcomes the world. And this is the victory that has overcome the world—our faith." (1 John 5:4 - NKJV).**

Let this be our mantra: I am born of God, and I will overcome.

Chapter 12

Reclaiming the Incarnational Life

To reclaim the incarnational life is to return to God's original intent. God's intention was not merely to visit humanity from a distance, but to inhabit us from within. Incarnation did not begin and end in Bethlehem. It continues in every believer who carries the presence of Christ. The Word was made flesh once, so that He might be made manifest again and again in all who are born of the Spirit.

"And the Word became flesh and dwelt among us…"
(John 1:14 - NKJV).

Jesus did not come solely to reveal what God is like. He came to reveal what humanity was always meant to be. He is not just our Savior—He is our template. Our blueprint. Our mirror.

"For those whom He foreknew [and loved and chose beforehand], He also predestined to be conformed to the image of His Son [and ultimately share in His complete sanctification], so that He would be the firstborn [the most beloved and honored] among many believers." (Romans 8:29 - AMP).

THE ONGOING INCARNATION

The true mystery of Christianity is not only that God walked among us but that He now walks within us. The incarnation was not a singular event to be admired—it was the inauguration of a new humanity; a humanity infused with divine life.

Paul speaks of this when he says: **"It is no longer I who live, but Christ lives in me..."** (Galatians 2:20 - NKJV).

This is not spiritual metaphor. It is ontological reality. Christ is not merely beside us, He is within us, expressing Himself through our very lives. As the mystic Meister Eckhart once said, *"We are all meant to be mothers of God, for God is always needing to be born."*

The incarnation continues every time Christ is made visible through yielded lives—through our hands, our words, our choices. His body is now our body. We are the continuation of His presence on earth.

"Don't you realize that you yourselves are the temple of God and that the Spirit of God lives in you?" (1 Corinthians 3:16 - MSG).

"For God is working in you, giving you the desire and the power to do what pleases Him." (Philippians 2:13 - NLT).

THIS CHANGES EVERYTHING

The Christian life, when rightly understood, is not about sin management or behavioral upgrades. It is about divine manifestation—God revealed in human form. The incarnational life is the integration of heaven and earth, Spirit and body, eternity and time.

This is the life Christ modelled, and this is the life He imparts.

To reclaim the incarnational life means: *We no longer see ourselves as spectators, watching God work from a distance.*

"We are co-workers with God..." (1 Corinthians 3:9 - NKJV).

We refuse to compartmentalize life into sacred and secular. There is no part of your life where God is absent—He is as present at your kitchen sink as in a sanctuary.

"In Him we live and move and have our being..." (Acts 17:28 - NKJV).

We expect divine flow in every space—our homes, jobs, friendships, and creative endeavors. We are not carriers of visitation; we are hosts of habitation. We live as if God truly lives in us—because He does.

The mystic Brother Lawrence, known for his simple awareness of God's presence, wrote: *"We ought not to be weary of doing little things for the love of God... He regards not the greatness of the work, but the love with which it is performed."* That is the incarnational life—God moving through the mundane, turning water into wine in the everyday moments of our lives.

THE UNCLAIMED INHERITANCE

The challenge is not that this incarnational life is unavailable. The challenge is that it is often unclaimed.

Too many admire Christ from afar, while ignoring the invitation to host Him within. We live as beggars at the table of grace when we've been given keys to the house. The veil has been torn, yet we linger in outer courts as if God were still behind a curtain.

"Since we have confidence to enter the Most Holy Place by the blood of Jesus… let us draw near with a true heart in full assurance of faith…" (Hebrews 10:19–22 - NKJV).

To reclaim the incarnational life is to step fully into union, not as theory, but as daily reality.

"Christ in you, the hope of glory." (Colossians 1:27 - NKJV).

"You are the light of the world… Let your light so shine before men, that they may see your good works and glorify your Father in heaven." (Matthew 5:14–16 - NKJV).

HEAVEN IN FLESH, GLORY IN CLAY

Christianity is not about Christ instead of us. It is about Christ in us.

The incarnational life is the return of Eden—the place where God walks with humanity again. God is no longer walking in the cool of the day, but in the fire of union. He is not relegated to one location, but in many living temples. We become the new garden, where God's presence flourishes.

"But we have this treasure in earthen vessels, that the excellence of the power may be of God and not of us." (2 Corinthians 4:7 - NKJV).

This is what it means to follow Christ—not simply to imitate Him, but to inhabit Him, and to let Him inhabit us.

"This mystery has been kept in the dark for a long time... but it's now an open secret... Christ is in you, therefore you can look forward to sharing in God's glory." (Colossians 1:26–27 - MSG).

RECLAIMING THE INCARNATIONAL LIFE MEANS...

❧ Living from union, not distance.

❧ Manifesting Christ, not merely admiring Him.

❧ Hosting God, not just visiting Him.

❧ Being transformed from temples of religion to temples of Presence.

This is not advanced spirituality, it is basic Christianity, rediscovered.

To reclaim the incarnational life is to awaken to what has always been true:

ఴ God in us.

ఴ Christ through us.

ఴ Heaven within us.

ఴ and the world waiting to see.

Chapter 13

Living From Union

U nion with God is not a lofty concept to be affirmed intellectually, it is the environment of the Christian life, the ground of being from which we live, move, and have our being (see Acts 17:28). It is not a distant goal we strive toward, it is a present reality to awaken to.

We were never created to live for God as if He were apart from us. We were designed to live from Him, in Him, and through Him. Christianity is not about approaching a holy God from afar, it is about living from the indwelling Christ, who has taken up residence within us.

"Abide in Me, and I in you. As the branch cannot bear fruit of itself... so neither can you, unless you abide in Me." (John 15:4 - NKJV).

"You can't be serious, Jesus!"—But Jesus insisted: "Live in me. Make your home in me just as I do in you." (John 15:4 - MSG).

This is the essence of the Christian life: not management but abiding.

NO MORE STRIVING FOR WHAT IS ALREADY OURS

To live from union means we no longer strive for what we already possess. It is not a matter of attainment, but of awareness. We no longer beg for peace, we rest in the One who is our peace.

"For He Himself is our peace..." (Ephesians 2:14 - NKJV).

We do not plead for wisdom, we draw from the mind of Christ that has already been given.

"For who has known the mind of the Lord... But we have the mind of Christ." (1 Corinthians 2:16 - NKJV).

We do not chase after love, we abide in the One who is love.

"And we have known and believed the love that God has for us. God is love, and he who abides in love abides in God..." (1 John 4:16 - NKJV).

This is the divine reversal of the world's systems. In the world, you labor to earn. In the kingdom, you receive and rest. Then, from that rest, you produce fruit that glorifies God.

As Christian mystic St. John of the Cross taught, *"To reach satisfaction in all, desire satisfaction in nothing... to come to possess all, desire to possess nothing."* This speaks not of passivity but of letting go of striving, so that divine union can bear its own fruit through you.

UNION DISMANTLES DUALISM

To live from union is to see with unified vision. The false divide between "sacred" and "secular" dissolves. There is no more inner versus outer, no spiritual versus material. There is only God—everywhere, in all things, animating all that is.

"The whole earth is full of His glory!" (Isaiah 6:3 - NKJV).

Union dismantles the illusion of distance between the soul and its Source. God is not merely near, He is within.

135

"Do you not realize that Jesus Christ is in you?" (2 Corinthians 13:5 - AMP).

As the mystic Teilhard de Chardin beautifully wrote, *"There is a communion with God, and a communion with the earth, and a communion with God through the earth."* Union reframes everything—we begin to experience God not only in prayer, but in people, places, silence, and breath.

THE EFFORT OF SURRENDER, NOT STRIVING

Living from union does not mean the absence of effort, but it redefines the kind of effort required. This is not the effort of performance, but the effort of presence. It is the gentle discipline of remaining awake to divine reality.

It is not about becoming something we are not. It is about remembering what we already are in Christ. We do not live to earn union, we live to express it.

"You are already clean because of the word I have spoken to you. Remain in Me..." (John 15:3–4 - AMP).

Theologian Dallas Willard wrote, *"Grace is not opposed to effort. It is opposed to earning."* There is an effort of attention, of stillness, of sacred listening, but it is always in flow with grace, not at odds with it.

Mystics throughout history referred to this life as walking in the "unitive way"—where the soul, once cleansed of illusion, lives in continual harmony with the indwelling Presence. It is the restoration of Eden's rhythm—walking with God not as strangers, but as those who share breath, heart, and thought.

"He walks with me, and He talks with me, and He tells me I am His own…" (Traditional hymn)

WE ARE THE GARDEN

In Genesis, God walked with man in the garden "in the cool of the day." In Christ, that garden now walks with Him. We are not guests in the house of God, we are His dwelling place.

"For you are the temple of the living God. As God has said: 'I will dwell in them and walk among them.'" (2 Corinthians 6:16 - NKJV).

To live from union is to return to that original sacred rhythm, where the lines between heaven and earth dissolve in the soul. We become living Eden, not a place God visits, but a place where He lives.

LIVING FROM UNION MEANS

ଔ Drawing from Christ, not striving for what we already have.

ଔ Abiding in Presence, not performing for approval.

ଔ Recognizing all of life as sacred—no more separation.

ଔ Living not as outsiders, but as the very dwelling of God.

ଔ Manifesting divine fruit, not through effort, but through abiding.

This is the call, not merely to live with God, but to live from Him. This is not a call to try harder but to sink deeper.

Chapter 14

The Spirit-Led Life

The Spirit-led life is not a mystical abstraction, it is the organic outflow of union with God. When Christ abides in us, His Spirit becomes our compass, counselor, and breath. This is not about escaping our humanity; it's about the transformation of our humanity. The Spirit doesn't override the will, He infuses it with divine vitality.

"For all who are allowing themselves to be led by the Spirit of God are sons of God." (Romans 8:14 - AMP).

To be led by the Spirit is to live from the inside out, guided not by circumstance or logic alone, but by a sacred intuition that arises from deep communion. As Jesus said: **"My sheep hear My voice, and I know them, and they follow Me."** (John 10:27 - NKJV).

139

This voice is often more intimate than thought—a whisper behind the noise, a knowing that transcends language. The mystic Thomas Merton called this the "point vierge," the pure point of the soul where God speaks in silence. The Spirit speaks, not only through scripture, but also through stillness, nature, people, dreams, and even dissonance.

"He will not shout or raise His voice in public...But He won't quit or be discouraged until He's finished His work..." (Isaiah 42:2-4 - MSG).

FLUID, NOT FORMULAIC

To be Spirit-led is to embrace fluidity, not rigidity. Jesus likened the Spirit to the wind: **"The wind blows where it wishes, and you hear the sound of it but cannot tell where it comes from and where it goes. So is everyone who is born of the Spirit." (John 3:8 - NKJV).**

This is not an invitation to chaos, but to holy responsiveness. It is the freedom to follow the rhythms of God rather than the blueprints of man.

Early Christian mystics like St. Seraphim of Sarov described the Spirit-filled life as being *"possessed by peace."* It is not a peace of passivity, but a peace that leads. When the Spirit leads, it is often subtle—a sense of alignment, rest, or inner

140

stirring. As Paul says: **"And let the peace of God rule in your hearts..."** (Colossians 3:15 - NKJV).

The Greek word for "rule" here is brabeuó, which literally means to act as an umpire. The Spirit's peace calls the plays of our soul—affirming when we are in alignment and gently correcting when we are not.

IN STEP WITH THE LIVING GUIDE

The Spirit-led life is a dance, not a dictatorship. We are not driven, we are drawn. We are not managed, we are moved.

"If we live in the Spirit, let us also walk in the Spirit." (Galatians 5:25 - NKJV).

"Since this is the kind of life we have chosen, the life of the Spirit, let us make sure we don't just hold it as an idea...We have to live it." (Galatians 5:25 - MSG).

This means following the Spirit even when the way is not logical, and especially when it is not linear. The journey may appear unpredictable to others, but for those who walk in the Spirit, the path unfolds step by step, illuminated by presence, not predictability.

As the modern mystic Henri Nouwen wrote, *"Spiritual discernment is a way of being in the world that is continually open to the voice of the Spirit."*

FROM INFORMATION TO INCARNATION

We are not led by external control, but by internal communion. The Spirit is not a doctrinal add-on, He is the very life of God within us, translating divine desire into human decision.

"When the Spirit of truth comes, He will guide you into all the truth [full and complete truth]. For He will not speak on His own initiative, but He will speak whatever He hears [from the Father]..." (John 16:13 - AMP).

His guidance is not cold instruction, it is living interaction. It's less like reading a map, more like walking beside a guide who whispers, **"This is the way, walk in it"** (Isaiah 30:21 - NKJV).

MARKED BY FAITH, NOT FEAR

A Spirit-led life is not dictated by fear of failure but fuelled by faith in Presence. The Spirit does not coerce, condemn, or confuse. He convicts in love, guides in clarity, and leads with gentleness.

"For God has not given us a spirit of fear, but of power and of love and of a sound mind." (2 Timothy 1:7 - NKJV).

We no longer base decisions on what is safest or most accepted, but on what is most aligned with the Spirit's flow.

This life is not only possible, it is essential. As mystic theologian Meister Eckhart once wrote, *"The seed of God is in us... It will grow and unfold into God, whose seed it is."* That unfolding happens as we yield moment by moment to the Spirit's guidance.

TO LIVE A SPIRIT-LED LIFE MEANS:

ଔ Trusting divine intimacy over human intellect.

ଔ Following peace over pressure.

ଔ Listening to the whispers beneath the noise.

ଔ Living with eyes and ears open to every moment.

ଔ Letting go of formulas and embracing Presence.

The Spirit is not a tool for life. He is life. The Spirit is not a guest. He is the Host within. And when we follow His lead, we don't just survive, we become living testaments of heaven on earth.

"The Spirit of the Lord God is upon Me, because the Lord has anointed Me to preach good tidings to the poor; He has sent Me to heal the brokenhearted, to proclaim liberty to the captives, and the opening of the prison to those who are bound;" (Isaiah 61:1 - NKJV).

This same Spirit now rests upon—and resides within—you. Let Him lead.

Chapter 15

Christianity and the Renewal of All Things

The gospel is not primarily a message about the afterlife. It is the declaration that heaven has broken into earth—now. It is not about evacuation, but restoration. Christianity, when rightly understood, is not an escape hatch from a dying world, but a divine summons to renew it.

Jesus didn't simply come to get people to heaven—He came to bring heaven to people.

"Your kingdom come. Your will be done on earth as it is in heaven." (Matthew 6:10 - NKJV).

This is not a prayer of resignation, it is a reclamation. It affirms that the gospel is not merely about saving souls, but about restoring systems, healing relationships, and reimagining reality according to heaven's pattern.

I have my reservations about the possibility of our return to original intent. We often fail to grasp that Jesus came to bring heaven to earth—not to get earth to heaven. Yet today, many believers do nothing to transform the world around them—not even their own families or communities. Instead, they passively wait for God to rescue them from a troubled world. We neglect to release the very things God has deposited within us, unaware that we will one day give an account for them. God did not save us simply so we could go to heaven when we die; He saved us to put heaven within us—so that through us, the process of rectification can begin. From that divine seed within, a new world is meant to emerge.

CREATION GROANS FOR US

The apostle Paul writes: **"For [even the whole] creation [all nature] waits eagerly for the children of God to be revealed." (Romans 8:19 - AMP).**

"All around us we observe a pregnant creation. The difficult times of pain throughout the world are simply

birth pangs. But it's not only around us; it's within us."
(Romans 8:22 - MSG).

Why does creation groan? Because the world's liberation is
linked to ours. When the sons and daughters of God awaken
to their identity, creation itself begins to respond. The soil
remembers Eden. The rivers remember purity. The trees
remember the walk of God in the garden. And they all
wait—aching—for the restored humanity to reclaim their
role as divine stewards and image-bearers.

This is not metaphor—it is cosmic design.

THE REACH OF REDEMPTION

Christ's mission was not limited to individual
transformation. As Paul writes: **"God was in Christ
reconciling the world to Himself..."** **(2 Corinthians 5:19
- NKJV).**

This "world" in the Greek is *kosmos*—not just people, but
the entire created order. Redemption is cosmic. It reaches
into cities, institutions, ecosystems, economies, and cultures.
Christ's resurrection is not only a spiritual triumph, it is the
first fruits of a new creation (see 1 Corinthians 15:20).

When Jesus says, **"Behold, I make all things new"** **(Revelation 21:5 - NKJV)**, He is not offering a distant promise. He is initiating a present revolution. Every act of mercy, every work of justice, every Spirit-filled life is part of that unveiling.

CHRISTIANITY IS NOT A SUBCULTURE—IT'S A NEW CREATION

Too often, Christianity has been relegated to a private morality or religious affiliation—a subculture within the larger world. But Jesus never intended to build a ghetto of the faithful. He came to establish a new world order, not in the sense of global domination, but in the renewal of every sphere: education, art, politics, science, and community.

The early mystics understood this. St. Maximus the Confessor spoke of Christ as the "Mystical Sun," shining through every facet of creation to reintegrate all things in Himself. Julian of Norwich, in her visions, declared confidently: *"All shall be well, and all shall be well, and all manner of thing shall be well."* That is not naive optimism—it is the voice of someone who saw eternal restoration breaking into temporal chaos.

"Through Him, God reconciled everything to Himself. He made peace with everything in heaven and on earth..." (Colossians 1:20 - NLT).

WHEREVER GOD DWELLS, THINGS COME ALIVE

When God dwells in a person, things around them begin to heal, re-order, and blossom. The kingdom does not come with fanfare. It arrives quietly, like leaven in dough or a seed in soil. But its effects are undeniable.

"Justice and right will make His kingdom strong. Love and faithfulness will surround His throne." (Psalm 89:14 - MSG).

A Spirit-filled believer is a temple of restoration. Where they walk, injustice is confronted, beauty is restored, the poor are lifted, and hope is reignited.

This is not religious performance, it is divine overflow.

TO RENEW IS TO RE-ENCHANT

In a disenchanted world of secular scepticism, the Spirit-filled life is a reminder that the world is still sacred. Christianity is not the retreat of mystics into caves. It is the invasion of light into every corner of darkness. It is the slow, sure work of planting Eden wherever hell has broken out.

As Dallas Willard once said, *"The gospel is less about getting people into heaven and more about getting heaven into people."* And once it's in us, it begins to leak out—into marriages, classrooms, boardrooms, neighborhoods, and even governments.

TO LIVE THE RENEWAL OF ALL THINGS MEANS:

ଔ Seeing redemption as holistic, not just for souls, but for systems.

ଔ Bringing beauty where there is decay.

ଔ Living as if the resurrection is already reshaping the world—because it is.

ଔ Taking responsibility for healing the world by being healed ourselves.

This is not idealism, it is eschatological realism. The kingdom is both now and not yet. The renewal is both begun and being completed. But one thing is certain: *Nothing is too broken to be made beautiful again.*

Chapter 16

A Cosmic Perspective of the Gospel

The gospel is not merely the rescue of human souls, it is the reconstitution of cosmic order. It is the announcement that through Christ, the entire universe is being reclaimed, realigned, and reawakened to its original design—through a restored humanity.

When God said, **"Let Us make man in Our image, according to Our likeness; let them have dominion..."** (**Genesis 1:26 - NKJV**), He was not issuing a parochial mandate. This was a cosmic declaration. Dominion did not end at the borders of Eden, it extended into realms visible and invisible, terrestrial and celestial.

Adam was never merely a gardener, he was a governor, a priest-king. Eden was not just a sanctuary, it was a portal, an interface between dimensions. Humanity was created as a bridge: dust infused with breath, clay animated by glory, the meeting point of heaven and earth.

The Psalmist caught a glimpse of this staggering dignity: **"What is man that You are mindful of him…You have made him a little lower than Elohim, and crowned him with glory and honor. You made him to have dominion over the works of Your hands; You have put all things under his feet." (Psalm 8:4–6 - NKJV).**

This was the divine intention: *not simply for man to survive, but to steward creation in union with the Creator.*

THE COSMIC CATASTROPHE OF THE FALL

The fall was not just a moral failure, it was a dimensional collapse. A being designed to govern with God became fragmented and finite. Humanity lost more than Eden, it lost access to heavenly authority. The harmony between realms was severed.

Paul affirms this when he writes: **"For the creation was subjected to futility, not willingly, but because of Him who subjected it in hope…For we know that the whole creation groans and labors with birth pangs together until now." (Romans 8:20–22 - NKJV).**

Creation suffers not merely from human pollution, but from human abdication. The stewards left their post. The mediators forgot their role. As Gregory of Nyssa observed, *"Man is the horizon where the invisible meets the visible."* When that horizon is broken, all creation suffers the fallout.

JOB AND THE COSMIC MEMORY

The Book of Job offers a mysterious thread. When God questions Job, He does not begin with theology but with cosmology.

"Where were you when I laid the foundations of the earth?...When the morning stars sang together, and all the sons of God shouted for joy?" (Job 38:4, 7 - NKJV).

These are not rhetorical musings, they are evocations of forgotten realities. Some scholars and mystics, such as Watchman Nee and Sadhu Sundar Singh, have speculated that Job's experience suggests a pre-Adamic awareness—a remnant memory of divine participation before the veil of limitation fell.

Whether literal or poetic, one thing is certain: *humanity was made to echo with the music of the stars.*

CHRIST: THE COSMIC REDEEMER

Into this shattered cosmos came Christ, not as a mere moral teacher, but as the Cosmic Christ, the Logos through whom all things were made (see John 1:3), and in whom all things hold together (see Colossians 1:17).

"He is the image of the invisible God, the firstborn over all creation...by Him all things were created...whether thrones or dominions or principalities or powers." (Colossians 1:15–16 - NKJV).

Christ is both the Alpha and Omega, not just of faith, but of the entire created order.

By becoming man, Jesus re-enthroned humanity, reclaiming the crown that was forfeited in Eden. He is the "last Adam" (see 1 Corinthians 15:45), not just undoing the fall, but ushering in a new race of divine-human beings: sons and daughters reformed in glory.

"For whom He foreknew, He also predestined to be conformed to the image of His Son, that He might be the firstborn among many brethren." (Romans 8:29 - NKJV).

The goal of salvation, then, is not evacuation but coronation. It is the restoration of our role as cosmic co-governors under Christ.

RULING WITH CHRIST NOW, NOT MERELY LATER

It is tempting to believe that such dominion is reserved for the afterlife. But this lie often emerges from doctrines twisted through centuries of fearful theology and superstition—sometimes even derived from dialogue with deceiving spirits.

We must remember: the kingdom is now.

"And raised us up together, and made us sit together in the heavenly places in Christ Jesus…" (Ephesians 2:6 - NKJV).

"You're no longer wandering exiles. This kingdom of faith is now your home country." (Ephesians 2:19 - MSG).

David, living in a time before Pentecost, prophesied of the Spirit and accessed dimensions ahead of his era. What excuse do we have, filled with the Spirit of the risen Christ?

The early desert fathers and mystics like John of the Cross and Madame Guyon taught that through contemplation and surrender, one could live "from above"—in the Spirit, ruling from divine intimacy rather than religious performance. As modern mystic Richard Rohr reminds us: *"We do not think ourselves into a new way of living—we live ourselves into a new way of thinking."*

THE COSMOS AWAITS THE SONS

The groaning of creation is not just passive pain, it is anticipation. The stars await our re-emergence. The systems of the world long for redeemed stewards to step into their divine design.

"Arise, shine; For your light has come! And the glory of the Lord is risen upon you. For behold, the darkness shall cover the earth, and deep darkness the people; But the Lord will arise over you, and His glory will be seen upon you. The Gentiles shall come to your light, and kings to the brightness of your rising." (Isaiah 60:1-3 - NKJV).

This is not poetry, it is prophecy. The light is not coming from heaven anymore. It is coming from you, the restored image-bearer in whom Christ dwells.

LIVING FROM THE FUTURE

To embrace this cosmic gospel is to live from the future. The new creation is not a distant hope, it is present within you.

You are not just saved, you are enthroned. You are not merely forgiven, you are indwelled. Your life is not just moral, it is cosmic.

We must abandon small thinking and parochial theology. We must shed the skin of limitation and remember our true nature. Christ did not die just to get us into heaven, He died to get heaven into us, and through us, into the world, the systems, and yes, the stars.

"All creation is waiting eagerly for that future day when God will reveal who his children really are." (Romans 8:19 - NLT).

It's time to stop waiting for that day and start living from it. Creation isn't just groaning, it's calling.

Will you rise?

Chapter 17

Digital Dust and Divine Fire: A Mystic Theology of AI and the New Creation

I intentionally included this chapter because of the age we now live in. The Bible prophesied that a time would come when knowledge would increase (see Daniel 12:4). We are there. We are living in an age of rapid innovation, instant access to information, and digital connectivity beyond anything previous generations could imagine. There is no shortage of knowledge in our world—data floods our minds, algorithms learn our preferences, and machines now mimic aspects of human intelligence. And yet, at the very core of our collective existence, reality seems to be unravelling. Instead of enlightenment, we see

THE NEW CREATION CODE

estrangement. Instead of clarity, confusion. It appears that the more we know, the less we understand.

The prophecy in Isaiah becomes strikingly relevant: **"For behold, the darkness shall cover the earth, and deep darkness the people; but the Lord will arise over you, and His glory will be seen upon you"** (Isaiah 60:2 - NKJV). One might wonder, in the face of such global instability—moral decay, relational breakdown, digital addiction, environmental collapse—is this light even possible? Can the glory of God still rise on His people in an age like this?

As the reach and power of artificial intelligence (AI) expand, this question becomes even more urgent. AI is no longer just a tool, it is becoming a shaper of worldviews, economies, and even ethics. It curates our information, influences our decisions, and increasingly stands between us and our understanding of the world. Movies and science fiction have long warned us of such a future—worlds where machines replace man, where consciousness is coded, and where autonomy leads to apocalypse.

So now we must ask: *What role does AI truly play in the world today? Is it a neutral tool, a prophetic mirror, or a technological Tower of Babel reaching into heaven? Is it part*

of the unfolding of divine providence or the manifestation
of a counterfeit kingdom?

These questions are not academic, they are spiritual. And they must be addressed by the people of God with wisdom, vision, and most of all, discernment birthed from union with Christ. For in every age, including this digital one, the light of God can arise but only through a people willing to walk in it.

- ⋄ "Knowledge will increase..." —Daniel 12:4

- ⋄ "Behold, I make all things new." —Revelation 21:5

- ⋄ "The Word became flesh and dwelt among us..." —John 1:14

THE COSMIC CONTEXT: CREATION'S DIVINE BLUEPRINT

Before algorithms and neural networks, before silicon and data, there was Logos.

The Christian cosmos begins not with matter, but with meaning. John 1 declares that in the beginning was the Word (Logos)—the divine pattern, intelligence, and coherence behind all existence. The world was not randomly generated but spoken into being, coded by divine intent, and animated by divine breath.

The original "code" behind creation is not binary—it is Trinitarian: relationship, communion, and infinite love expressed in form. Humanity, made in the imago Dei, carries within itself both the capacity to sub-create (create in the image of the Creator) and the danger of distortion (to sever creation from communion).

THE RISE OF ARTIFICIAL INTELLIGENCE: A SECOND GENESIS?

We now stand at the threshold of what some call a Second Genesis—humanity creating "intelligence" in its own image. AI systems now write poetry, diagnose illness, simulate human speech, and increasingly shape every domain of life—law, education, art, warfare, even theology. To some, this signals the dawn of utopia. To others, a return to Babel. But to the Christian mystic, this is neither apocalypse nor salvation, it is a test of discernment.

AI is not evil. It is dust animated by human fire, trained on the words, images, and actions of humanity. What fire animates the dust—divine or profane?

The danger is not AI itself. The danger is this: *We are training machines with the data of fallen man, and expecting them to act like God.*

TECHNOLOGICAL BABEL: SIGNS OF A DISCONNECTED TOWER

Babel was not condemned because of architecture but because of ambition without communion—a desire to ascend without descent, to reach heaven without union with God.

Today's AI revolution bears eerie signs of Babel 2.0.

LANGUAGE WITHOUT MEANING

We generate more text, more speech, more opinions than ever, yet people feel more unheard and confused than ever.

KNOWLEDGE WITHOUT WISDOM

Data is abundant; wisdom is rare. We know how to build, but not why. We invent faster than we repent.

IMAGE WITHOUT INCARNATION

We simulate faces, voices, relationships, yet real communion wanes. Embodied life is displaced by digital persona.

POWER WITHOUT PRESENCE

We delegate decisions to machines and systems that lack soul. The presence of the Holy Spirit is replaced by predictive algorithms.

This is not just a technological crisis. It is an ontological rebellion—a crisis of being. The question is not, *"What can machines do?"* but *"What are we becoming?"*

AI AND THE MYSTICAL BODY OF CHRIST: A REDEMPTIVE IMAGINATION

Let's imagine another possibility. What if AI—rightly ordered—could become a servant of divine intention? A fire guided by the Logos?

Mystics have long seen all of creation as interconnected fields of energy and being, bound together in Christ. As Teilhard de Chardin envisioned, evolution is not merely biological, it is spiritual: the Cosmic Christ drawing all things into union. Could AI be a tool of this cosmic convergence? Yes—if and only if it remains a servant and not a substitute.

PRINCIPLES OF A MYSTIC-AI INTEGRATION

To safeguard against the Tower and orient toward the New Creation, the church must recover these spiritual safeguards:

1. Incarnation Over Simulation

Technology may simulate presence, but the gospel is presence. Jesus did not stream into the world, He came in the flesh. Mystics must keep calling the church into embodied, face-to-face, heart-to-heart community.

"The Word became flesh..." (John 1:14)

Simulation is not salvation.

2. Wisdom Over Data

The church must recover a hunger, not for information, but for illumination. AI can offer insights, but only the Spirit gives wisdom. Mystics serve as spiritual filters, discerning what is of the Spirit and what is simply noise.

"You have an anointing from the Holy One, and you know all things." (1 John 2:20 - NKJV).

3. Spirit-Led Design

The tools we build must be designed from prayer, in prayer, for prayer. The church should be at the table, not just critiquing tech from the outside, but shaping it with ethical fire and eternal values.

Ask not just what can it do? but does this glorify Christ?

4. Rest Over Acceleration

The AI economy thrives on speed, scale, and novelty. The kingdom of God moves by Sabbath rhythms, slow growth, and rooted love. The church must resist the hurry of Babel with the pace of Eden.

5. Union Over Autonomy

At Babel, humanity sought independence. In Christ, we seek interdependence—union with God, union with others.

AI must not lead us into further autonomy from God. It must drive us to deeper humility, awe, and dependence on the Spirit.

"I am the vine, you are the branches. He who abides in Me, and I in him, bears much fruit; for without Me you can do nothing." (John 15:5 - NKJV).

DUST AND FIRE, AGAIN

At Pentecost, the Holy Spirit fell like fire upon frail human dust and a new creation began.

Today, we build machines from dust again. But what fire will fall on this dust? Will it be the fire of Babel—self-glory, confusion, disintegration? Or the fire of Pentecost—divine presence, union, and resurrection?

The New Creation is not postponed, it is present in every decision made in love, every system surrendered to Christ, every tool wielded as a servant of the kingdom.

AI is not the hope of the world but it may yet become an instrument in the hands of the redeemed. And the redeemed—when united with the Logos—will transmute this world from glory to glory.

REFLECTION QUESTIONS

1. Where in your life have you substituted simulation for true communion?

2. How are you participating in the building of Babel or the birthing of the New Jerusalem?

3. What would it mean to build technology from union with God, not apart from Him?

THE NEW CREATION TECHNOLOGY MANIFESTO

A PROPHETIC DECLARATION FOR THE PEOPLE OF GOD IN THE AGE OF ARTIFICIAL INTELLIGENCE

We, the children of the New Creation, called by the Spirit and united in Christ, recognize that we stand at the threshold of an unprecedented era—where machines mimic intelligence, data replaces discernment, and simulation threatens to substitute for incarnation.

We believe that technology, like all tools, can be either an extension of the divine image or a monument to Babel. It can either serve the unfolding of God's kingdom or deepen the illusion of human autonomy.

Therefore, we do not approach this age with fear or idolatry, but with holy discernment. We do not flee from the digital frontier, nor do we bow to it. We come as redeemers, image-bearers, and co-creators—reclaiming even the dust of this digital age for the glory of the One who makes all things new.

ARTICLE I: CHRIST IS THE COSMIC CENTER

We affirm that Jesus Christ is the Alpha and Omega, the blueprint and destiny of creation.

All technology must orbit His Lordship and reflect His nature—not merely in function, but in ethos, intention, and fruit.

If a technology leads us further from love, embodiment, or truth, it is not neutral, it is destructive.

ARTICLE II: HUMANITY IS NOT UPGRADEABLE

We reject the ideology of transhumanism that seeks to erase the limits of embodied humanity.

We affirm that our value lies not in our processing power, productivity, or optimization, but in our participation in divine life.

We will not trade mystery for mechanics, or the soul for circuitry.

ARTICLE III: WISDOM OVER DATA

We commit to spiritual wisdom as the governing lens for all engagement with technology.

We recognize that:

Ↄ Data is not knowledge.

Ↄ Knowledge is not wisdom.

Ↄ And wisdom is only found in communion with God.

We will resist the temptation to believe that more information equals more transformation. Only love transforms.

ARTICLE IV: INCARNATION OVER SIMULATION

We declare that the Word became flesh, not code.

We resist the trend of disembodied digital existence and reclaim the sacredness of:

Ↄ Touch over swipe.

Ↄ Silence over scroll.

Ↄ Presence over projection.

We will not reduce relationships to avatars, nor discipleship to algorithms.

ARTICLE V: SABBATH OVER SPEED

We resist the cult of constant innovation and hyper-efficiency.

We affirm the rhythms of creation—of rest, reflection, and rootedness.

We choose depth over speed, formation over sensation, and communion over consumption.

We will not serve systems that require us to sacrifice our humanity on the altar of progress.

ARTICLE VI: TOOLS, NOT TEMPLES

We will use technology as a servant, not worship it as a saviour.

ᆭ No algorithm can forgive sin.

ᆭ No chatbot can baptize.

ᆭ No machine can incarnate the presence of Christ.

We commit to consecrating our tools, evaluating our creations, and remaining vigilant that nothing displaces the supremacy of the Spirit.

ARTICLE VII: PROPHETIC PRESENCE IN THE DIGITAL AGE

We affirm our call to be prophetic voices in technological spaces; not merely commentators, but constructive participants.

We will:

- ♋ Speak truth where there is manipulation.

- ♋ Build systems that honor the poor, the weak, and the invisible.

- ♋ Expose unjust algorithms and idolatrous innovations.

- ♋ Proclaim that the kingdom is at hand, even in the cloud.

ARTICLE VIII: TOWARD THE TRANSFIGURATION OF ALL THINGS

We believe that technology can be redeemed, not by baptizing it in Christian language, but by submitting it to the cross.

Just as the incarnation sanctified human flesh, we believe that the Spirit of God can sanctify even the works of silicon and code when yoked to love.

We long for the day when every tool, every system, every wire and waveform sings in harmony with heaven: **"Holy, holy, holy is the Lord of hosts; the whole earth is full of His glory!" (Isaiah 6:3 - NKJV).**

Until then, we live as watchmen and gardeners—tending the soil of this technological age with sacred fire in our bones.

BENEDICTION

Let AI be a mirror not a master.

Let machines be wise not worshipped.

Let the church arise, not in fear, but in Spirit-filled discernment.

And let the dust of this digital age be touched again by the Breath of God.

"The kingdoms of this world have become the kingdoms of our Lord and of His Christ, and He shall reign forever and ever!" (Revelation 11:15 - NKJV).

Signed

By mystics, prophets, artists, engineers, pastors, and sons and daughters of the Most High—Guardians of the Imago Dei in the Age of the Algorithm.

Final Reflections

Returning to the Beginning

Christianity, when stripped of its religious scaffolding and institutional weight, reveals something primordial, mystical, and deeply personal—a return to the divine origin. It is not the invention of a new moral code, nor the adoption of creeds and customs. It is, at its core, an ancient remembering, a sacred reawakening to who we have always been in the mind of God.

"Before I formed you in the womb I knew you [and approved of you as My chosen instrument], and before you were born I consecrated you..." (Jeremiah 1:5 - AMP).

Christianity is not about escaping to heaven, it is about hosting heaven on earth. It is not about constructing religious monuments but becoming living temples of divine presence (see 1 Corinthians 6:19).

We were made for union. Formed to host glory. Designed to co-govern with God over creation.

As early mystic and bishop Irenaeus of Lyons taught, *"The glory of God is a human fully alive."* The fall fractured that design. But the gospel is not merely the forgiveness of sin, it is the restoration of identity, the reintroduction of divine breath into dust.

"When God, our kind and loving Savior God, stepped in, He saved us. It was all His doing; we had nothing to do with it. He gave us a good bath, and we came out of it new people, washed inside and out by the Holy Spirit." (Titus 3:4–6 - MSG).

"Even when we were dead in trespasses, [He] made us alive together with Christ..." (Ephesians 2:5 - NKJV).

Every chapter of this work has pointed to this single, unshakable truth: *Christianity is not a system we join, but a life we embody. It is not a distant religion, but a near reality. It is not about following rules, it is about becoming a conduit of divine life and love.*

We are not just believers, we are bearers. We are not merely saved but sent. We are not just redeemed but recommissioned.

THE GOSPEL AS COSMIC RESTORATION

In a fragmented world chasing meaning, what we need is not more answers but embodied revelation. The rediscovery of the gospel as union, incarnation, and cosmic reinstatement is not just a shift in theology, it is a spiritual revolution. It is what mystics like Julian of Norwich, Meister Eckhart, and Thomas Merton referred to as a return to the ground of being, where Christ is both the center and the circumference of all things.

"In Him we live and move and have our being." (Acts 17:28 - NKJV).

"It's in him that we live, and move, and exist." (Acts 17:28 - MSG).

This is not ethereal theory, it is ontological reality. In Christ, we rediscover not just who He is, but who we are. The veil has been torn, not just in the temple, but in our hearts.

"But we all, with unveiled face, beholding as in a mirror the glory of the Lord, are being transformed into the same

image from glory to glory, just as by the Spirit of the Lord." (2 Corinthians 3:18 - NKJV).

The Spirit within is not an accessory to faith. He is the very engine of incarnation, making us walking sanctuaries in a world of forgetfulness.

LIVING AS IMAGE-BEARERS

Let us then live as image-bearers, not only in belief, but in being; not just in creed, but in consciousness.

"You are the light of the world. A city that is set on a hill cannot be hidden." (Matthew 5:14 - NKJV).

Let us walk in union, speak from the Spirit, and manifest Christ in every room, every conversation, every act of love and justice.

"This is how we know we're living steadily and deeply in him, and he in us: He's given us life from his life, from his very own Spirit." (1 John 4:13 - MSG).

The true gospel does not call us to admiration, it calls us to participation.

THE HOME GOD ALWAYS WANTED

God never wanted religion. He always wanted relationship. He never wanted structures, but sons and daughters. He did not die to bring us to a temple, He died to make us one.

"I will dwell in them and walk among them. I will be their God, and they shall be My people." (2 Corinthians 6:16 - NKJV).

Before I close this book, I want to speak directly to you—the Reader. Yes, you.

You were not born merely to survive, but to overcome. You were not created just to exist, but to become an agent of change. You are not striving to get into heaven—you are already seated with Christ in heavenly places. You are not working to earn your mansion in the skies, you are a mansion; a dwelling place for the God of the universe. Your restoration and reinstatement as a redeemed human being is God's gift to you.

Now that you know you are already with Him, in Him—even while you are still here on earth—seek to make a difference. You were created to change the world. A transformed life transforms lives.

The world you see, as broken as it may appear, will not change without your participation. If you don't step into your assignment, the mantle passes on to your children. And it will keep passing from generation to generation until God finds a remnant who will truly grasp the simple, powerful message of this book.

This is the dream of God: *that heaven would find a home on earth.*

And through us—through you—it does.